TEACHER'S PET PUBLICATIONS

PUZZLE PACK
for
A Streetcar Named Desire

based on the play by
Tennessee Williams

Written by
Mary B. Collins

© 2007 Teacher's Pet Publications
All Rights Reserved

The materials in this packet are copyrighted
by Teacher's Pet Publications, Inc.

These pages may be duplicated by the purchaser
for use in the purchaser's own classroom.

Copying any of these materials and distributing them
for any other purpose is a violation of the copyright laws.

© 2008 Teacher's Pet Publications, Inc.
www.tpet.com

INTRODUCTION
If you already own the LitPlan for this title, this Puzzle Pack will refresh your Unit Resource Materials and Vocabulary Resource Materials sections plus give you additional materials you can substitute into the tests. If you do not already have a complete LitPlan, these pages will give you some supplemental materials to use with your own plan. There are two main groups of materials: one set for unit words (such as characters' names, symbols, places, etc.) and one set for vocabulary words associated with the book.

WORD LIST
There is a word list for both the unit words and the vocabulary words. These lists show you which words are being used in the materials and the clues or definitions being used for those words. You may want to give students a word list with clues/definitions to help them, or you may want students to only have a word list (without clues/definitions) if you want them to work a little harder. Both are available for duplication. The word lists can also be your "calling key" for the bingo games.

FILL IN THE BLANK AND MATCHING
There are 4 each of the fill in the blank and matching worksheets for both the unit and vocabulary words. These pages can be used either as extra worksheets for students or as objective parts of a unit test. They can be done individually if students need extra help or as a whole class activity to review the material covered.

MAGIC SQUARES
The magic squares not only reinforce the material covered but also work on reasoning and math skills. Many teachers have told us that their students really enjoy doing these!

WORD SEARCH PUZZLES
The word search words go in all directions, as indicated on your answer keys. Two of the word search puzzles have the clues listed rather than the words. This makes the puzzle a little more difficult, but it reinforces the material better. Two word search puzzles have words only for students who find the clue puzzles too difficult.

CROSSWORD PUZZLES
Both unit and vocabulary word sections have 4 crossword puzzles.

BINGO CARDS
There are 32 individual bingo cards for the unit words and 32 individual bingo cards for the vocabulary words. You can use your word list as a "call list," calling the words at random and marking them off of your list as you go, or you could use the flash cards by cutting them apart and drawing the words at random from a hat (or box or whatever). To make a better review, you might ask for the definition and spelling of each word as you call it out–or you could call out the definitions and have students tell you the words they need to look for on the puzzle.

JUGGLE LETTERS
The vocabulary juggle letter game is intended to help students learn the spellings of the words. One sheet has the definitions listed on it as an extra help for students who need it or to reinforce the definitions if you choose to do so.

FLASH CARDS
We've included a set of vocabulary flash cards you can duplicate, cut, and fold for your students. Some teachers make a few sets for general use by the class; others make a set for each student. Some teachers duplicate them for each student and have the students cut & fold their own. You can cut out just the words and put them in a hat, have each student pick out one word and write the definition and a sentence for that word. Students then swap words and papers, with the next student adding a sentence of his own under the last one. You can have students swap as many times as you like. Each time the student will read the sentences written prior to his own and then add a sentence. You can cut out the words and definitions separately and play "I Have; Who Has?" Each student in the room draws a word and definition. The first student says, "I have (the name of the word). Who has the definition?" The student with the definition reads it then says, "I have (the name of the vocabulary word she has). Who has the definition?" The round continues until all words and definitions have been given.

A Streetcar Named Desire Word List

No.	Word	Clue/Definition
1.	ALLAN	He took his own life.
2.	APPEARANCE	According to Stella, this is Blanche's weakness.
3.	ARMS	Blanche renames the Flamingo The Tarantula ___ Hotel.
4.	ASYLUM	Blanche's destination
5.	BELLE	Lost plantation: ___ Reve
6.	BLANCHE	She ends up being sent to an institution.
7.	BOTTLE	Blanche physically threatens Stanley with a broken one.
8.	BUTTONS	Blanche asks Stanley for help with these.
9.	CIGARETTE	Mitch's ___ case was from a former girlfriend.
10.	CODE	Stanley says spousal ownership of property is the Napoleonic ___.
11.	CORN	In Stanley's joke, the rooster stopped pursuing the hen because of this.
12.	DEED	Proves home ownership
13.	ELYSIAN	Ironic apartment name; ___ Fields
14.	EUNICE	She accuses Steve of having an affair.
15.	FIRE	The word Blanche screams
16.	FLAMINGO	Cheap hotel of ill repute from which Blanche was asked to leave
17.	FLOWERS	The Mexican woman sells these.
18.	GRAPES	Blanche says eating unwashed ___ will cause her to die.
19.	HAROLD	Mitch's real name
20.	HOSPITAL	Stella is rushed there.
21.	ILLUSION	A woman's charm is fifty percent this.
22.	LANTERN	Stanley asks Blanche if she wants to take her paper one with her.
23.	LEAVING	It would make Blanche weep with joy.
24.	LETTERS	Blanche says she'll burn these that Stanley has touched.
25.	LIFE	According to Eunice, it keeps on going.
26.	LIGHTBULBS	Stanley smashed these on the wedding night.
27.	MITCH	He dumped Blanche when he found out about her past.
28.	MOTH	Williams compares Blanche's manner and clothing to this.
29.	MUSIC	Blanche hears this, which is not actually playing.
30.	PIG	Stella calls Stanley a ___.
31.	PLEIADES	Blanche seeks this in the sky.
32.	POE	Blanche says only he could describe the Kowalskis' living conditions.
33.	POKER	Game Stanley and the men played
34.	POLISH	Stanley's ethnic heritage
35.	PREGNANT	Stella's condition
36.	QUEENS	Stella and Blanche are referred to as a pair of ___.
37.	RADIO	Stanley threw it out the window.
38.	RHINESTONES	False gems
39.	SETTING	New Orleans
40.	SHAW	He knows the gossip about Blanche.
41.	SHEP	Blanche said he sent a telegram.
42.	SILK	Wedding night pajamas were made of this
43.	STANLEY	He rapes Blanche.
44.	STELLA	Blanche's sister; Stanley's wife
45.	STRANGERS	Blanche depended on the kindness of ___.
46.	STREETCAR	It is named Desire.

A Streetcar Named Desire Word List

No.	Word	Clue/Definition
47.	TIARA	At the start of Scene 10 Blanche wears a white evening gown, slippers, and this.
48.	TICKET	Stanley buys Blanche one for her birthday.
49.	VIRGO	Blanche's astrological sign
50.	WHITE	Meaning of Blanche's name
51.	WILLIAMS	Author
52.	WOOD	The name DuBois means this.

A Streetcar Named Desire Fill In The Blanks 1

1. Proves home ownership
2. The name DuBois means this.
3. Stella is rushed there.
4. Blanche physically threatens Stanley with a broken one.
5. Stella's condition
6. The Mexican woman sells these.
7. Blanche's sister; Stanley's wife
8. False gems
9. Game Stanley and the men played
10. It is named Desire.
11. Wedding night pajamas were made of this
12. Stanley asks Blanche if she wants to take her paper one with her.
13. He dumped Blanche when he found out about her past.
14. Blanche renames the Flamingo The Tarantula ___ Hotel.
15. Author
16. In Stanley's joke, the rooster stopped pursuing the hen because of this.
17. Stanley buys Blanche one for her birthday.
18. A woman's charm is fifty percent this.
19. Mitch's real name
20. Blanche depended on the kindness of ___.

A Streetcar Named Desire Fill In The Blanks 1 Answer Key

Answer	#	Clue
DEED	1.	Proves home ownership
WOOD	2.	The name DuBois means this.
HOSPITAL	3.	Stella is rushed there.
BOTTLE	4.	Blanche physically threatens Stanley with a broken one.
PREGNANT	5.	Stella's condition
FLOWERS	6.	The Mexican woman sells these.
STELLA	7.	Blanche's sister; Stanley's wife
RHINESTONES	8.	False gems
POKER	9.	Game Stanley and the men played
STREETCAR	10.	It is named Desire.
SILK	11.	Wedding night pajamas were made of this
LANTERN	12.	Stanley asks Blanche if she wants to take her paper one with her.
MITCH	13.	He dumped Blanche when he found out about her past.
ARMS	14.	Blanche renames the Flamingo The Tarantula ___ Hotel.
WILLIAMS	15.	Author
CORN	16.	In Stanley's joke, the rooster stopped pursuing the hen because of this.
TICKET	17.	Stanley buys Blanche one for her birthday.
ILLUSION	18.	A woman's charm is fifty percent this.
HAROLD	19.	Mitch's real name
STRANGERS	20.	Blanche depended on the kindness of ___.

A Streetcar Named Desire Fill In The Blanks 2

_____ 1. The word Blanche screams

_____ 2. Blanche's astrological sign

_____ 3. The Mexican woman sells these.

_____ 4. Blanche hears this, which is not actually playing.

_____ 5. Stanley says spousal ownership of property is the Napoleonic ___.

_____ 6. Stanley threw it out the window.

_____ 7. Proves home ownership

_____ 8. Stanley's ethnic heritage

_____ 9. Blanche seeks this in the sky.

_____ 10. Blanche says she'll burn these that Stanley has touched.

_____ 11. Author

_____ 12. False gems

_____ 13. It would make Blanche weep with joy.

_____ 14. At the start of Scene 10 Blanche wears a white evening gown, slippers, and this.

_____ 15. Blanche depended on the kindness of ___.

_____ 16. Stanley asks Blanche if she wants to take her paper one with her.

_____ 17. She accuses Steve of having an affair.

_____ 18. Wedding night pajamas were made of this

_____ 19. Blanche says only he could describe the Kowalskis' living conditions.

_____ 20. Blanche's sister; Stanley's wife

A Streetcar Named Desire Fill In The Blanks 2 Answer Key

FIRE	1. The word Blanche screams
VIRGO	2. Blanche's astrological sign
FLOWERS	3. The Mexican woman sells these.
MUSIC	4. Blanche hears this, which is not actually playing.
CODE	5. Stanley says spousal ownership of property is the Napoleonic ___.
RADIO	6. Stanley threw it out the window.
DEED	7. Proves home ownership
POLISH	8. Stanley's ethnic heritage
PLEIADES	9. Blanche seeks this in the sky.
LETTERS	10. Blanche says she'll burn these that Stanley has touched.
WILLIAMS	11. Author
RHINESTONES	12. False gems
LEAVING	13. It would make Blanche weep with joy.
TIARA	14. At the start of Scene 10 Blanche wears a white evening gown, slippers, and this.
STRANGERS	15. Blanche depended on the kindness of ___.
LANTERN	16. Stanley asks Blanche if she wants to take her paper one with her.
EUNICE	17. She accuses Steve of having an affair.
SILK	18. Wedding night pajamas were made of this
POE	19. Blanche says only he could describe the Kowalskis' living conditions.
STELLA	20. Blanche's sister; Stanley's wife

A Streetcar Named Desire Fill In The Blanks 3

1. New Orleans
2. Stanley's ethnic heritage
3. The Mexican woman sells these.
4. In Stanley's joke, the rooster stopped pursuing the hen because of this.
5. Stanley asks Blanche if she wants to take her paper one with her.
6. The word Blanche screams
7. At the start of Scene 10 Blanche wears a white evening gown, slippers, and this.
8. Cheap hotel of ill repute from which Blanche was asked to leave
9. Proves home ownership
10. Stella calls Stanley a ___.
11. The name DuBois means this.
12. A woman's charm is fifty percent this.
13. He rapes Blanche.
14. Blanche hears this, which is not actually playing.
15. It would make Blanche weep with joy.
16. Ironic apartment name; ___ Fields
17. Blanche asks Stanley for help with these.
18. Williams compares Blanche's manner and clothing to this.
19. Stanley says spousal ownership of property is the Napoleonic ___.
20. He took his own life.

A Streetcar Named Desire Fill In The Blanks 3 Answer Key

SETTING	1. New Orleans
POLISH	2. Stanley's ethnic heritage
FLOWERS	3. The Mexican woman sells these.
CORN	4. In Stanley's joke, the rooster stopped pursuing the hen because of this.
LANTERN	5. Stanley asks Blanche if she wants to take her paper one with her.
FIRE	6. The word Blanche screams
TIARA	7. At the start of Scene 10 Blanche wears a white evening gown, slippers, and this.
FLAMINGO	8. Cheap hotel of ill repute from which Blanche was asked to leave
DEED	9. Proves home ownership
PIG	10. Stella calls Stanley a ___.
WOOD	11. The name DuBois means this.
ILLUSION	12. A woman's charm is fifty percent this.
STANLEY	13. He rapes Blanche.
MUSIC	14. Blanche hears this, which is not actually playing.
LEAVING	15. It would make Blanche weep with joy.
ELYSIAN	16. Ironic apartment name; ___ Fields
BUTTONS	17. Blanche asks Stanley for help with these.
MOTH	18. Williams compares Blanche's manner and clothing to this.
CODE	19. Stanley says spousal ownership of property is the Napoleonic ___.
ALLAN	20. He took his own life.

Copyrighted

A Streetcar Named Desire Fill In The Blanks 4

1. He rapes Blanche.
2. Cheap hotel of ill repute from which Blanche was asked to leave
3. Stanley buys Blanche one for her birthday.
4. The Mexican woman sells these.
5. He dumped Blanche when he found out about her past.
6. Blanche renames the Flamingo The Tarantula ___ Hotel.
7. Blanche physically threatens Stanley with a broken one.
8. Stanley's ethnic heritage
9. Blanche depended on the kindness of ___.
10. Lost plantation: ___ Reve
11. Meaning of Blanche's name
12. Stanley threw it out the window.
13. Blanche says eating unwashed ___ will cause her to die.
14. She ends up being sent to an institution.
15. Stanley smashed these on the wedding night.
16. Stella is rushed there.
17. She accuses Steve of having an affair.
18. He knows the gossip about Blanche.
19. Ironic apartment name; ___ Fields
20. A woman's charm is fifty percent this.

A Streetcar Named Desire Fill In The Blanks 4 Answer Key

STANLEY	1. He rapes Blanche.
FLAMINGO	2. Cheap hotel of ill repute from which Blanche was asked to leave
TICKET	3. Stanley buys Blanche one for her birthday.
FLOWERS	4. The Mexican woman sells these.
MITCH	5. He dumped Blanche when he found out about her past.
ARMS	6. Blanche renames the Flamingo The Tarantula ___ Hotel.
BOTTLE	7. Blanche physically threatens Stanley with a broken one.
POLISH	8. Stanley's ethnic heritage
STRANGERS	9. Blanche depended on the kindness of ___.
BELLE	10. Lost plantation: ___ Reve
WHITE	11. Meaning of Blanche's name
RADIO	12. Stanley threw it out the window.
GRAPES	13. Blanche says eating unwashed ___ will cause her to die.
BLANCHE	14. She ends up being sent to an institution.
LIGHTBULBS	15. Stanley smashed these on the wedding night.
HOSPITAL	16. Stella is rushed there.
EUNICE	17. She accuses Steve of having an affair.
SHAW	18. He knows the gossip about Blanche.
ELYSIAN	19. Ironic apartment name; ___ Fields
ILLUSION	20. A woman's charm is fifty percent this.

A Streetcar Named Desire Matching 1

___ 1. EUNICE
___ 2. FIRE
___ 3. LIGHTBULBS
___ 4. POKER
___ 5. SILK
___ 6. BOTTLE
___ 7. BELLE
___ 8. ELYSIAN
___ 9. STRANGERS
___ 10. BUTTONS
___ 11. WHITE
___ 12. VIRGO
___ 13. CIGARETTE
___ 14. APPEARANCE
___ 15. POE
___ 16. GRAPES
___ 17. PIG
___ 18. MUSIC
___ 19. LIFE
___ 20. STANLEY
___ 21. BLANCHE
___ 22. QUEENS
___ 23. LANTERN
___ 24. RHINESTONES
___ 25. ILLUSION

A. False gems
B. Stella and Blanche are referred to as a pair of ___.
C. Lost plantation: ___ Reve
D. According to Eunice, it keeps on going.
E. Wedding night pajamas were made of this
F. Meaning of Blanche's name
G. She accuses Steve of having an affair.
H. Blanche's astrological sign
I. She ends up being sent to an institution.
J. Blanche hears this, which is not actually playing.
K. Ironic apartment name; ___ Fields
L. Mitch's ____ case was from a former girlfriend.
M. Stanley asks Blanche if she wants to take her paper one with her.
N. The word Blanche screams
O. Blanche says only he could describe the Kowalskis' living conditions.
P. Stanley smashed these on the wedding night.
Q. Game Stanley and the men played
R. Blanche physically threatens Stanley with a broken one.
S. Blanche says eating unwashed ___ will cause her to die.
T. A woman's charm is fifty percent this.
U. Blanche depended on the kindness of ___.
V. Stella calls Stanley a ___.
W. Blanche asks Stanley for help with these.
X. According to Stella, this is Blanche's weakness.
Y. He rapes Blanche.

A Streetcar Named Desire Matching 1 Answer Key

G - 1. EUNICE	A. False gems
N - 2. FIRE	B. Stella and Blanche are referred to as a pair of ___.
P - 3. LIGHTBULBS	C. Lost plantation: ___ Reve
Q - 4. POKER	D. According to Eunice, it keeps on going.
E - 5. SILK	E. Wedding night pajamas were made of this
R - 6. BOTTLE	F. Meaning of Blanche's name
C - 7. BELLE	G. She accuses Steve of having an affair.
K - 8. ELYSIAN	H. Blanche's astrological sign
U - 9. STRANGERS	I. She ends up being sent to an institution.
W -10. BUTTONS	J. Blanche hears this, which is not actually playing.
F - 11. WHITE	K. Ironic apartment name; ___ Fields
H -12. VIRGO	L. Mitch's ___ case was from a former girlfriend.
L - 13. CIGARETTE	M. Stanley asks Blanche if she wants to take her paper one with her.
X -14. APPEARANCE	N. The word Blanche screams
O -15. POE	O. Blanche says only he could describe the Kowalskis' living conditions.
S -16. GRAPES	P. Stanley smashed these on the wedding night.
V -17. PIG	Q. Game Stanley and the men played
J - 18. MUSIC	R. Blanche physically threatens Stanley with a broken one.
D -19. LIFE	S. Blanche says eating unwashed ___ will cause her to die.
Y -20. STANLEY	T. A woman's charm is fifty percent this.
I - 21. BLANCHE	U. Blanche depended on the kindness of ___.
B -22. QUEENS	V. Stella calls Stanley a ___.
M -23. LANTERN	W. Blanche asks Stanley for help with these.
A -24. RHINESTONES	X. According to Stella, this is Blanche's weakness.
T -25. ILLUSION	Y. He rapes Blanche.

Copyrighted

A Streetcar Named Desire Matching 2

___ 1. WHITE
___ 2. BLANCHE
___ 3. GRAPES
___ 4. POKER
___ 5. STELLA
___ 6. MITCH
___ 7. WOOD
___ 8. HAROLD
___ 9. MOTH
___ 10. ILLUSION
___ 11. TIARA
___ 12. VIRGO
___ 13. STRANGERS
___ 14. LIGHTBULBS
___ 15. SETTING
___ 16. ASYLUM
___ 17. SHEP
___ 18. STREETCAR
___ 19. QUEENS
___ 20. DEED
___ 21. PIG
___ 22. BOTTLE
___ 23. ALLAN
___ 24. EUNICE
___ 25. MUSIC

A. Blanche says eating unwashed ___ will cause her to die.
B. Stanley smashed these on the wedding night.
C. Blanche's sister; Stanley's wife
D. Blanche physically threatens Stanley with a broken one.
E. Stella and Blanche are referred to as a pair of ___.
F. New Orleans
G. Blanche's astrological sign
H. Blanche hears this, which is not actually playing.
I. It is named Desire.
J. Blanche's destination
K. Proves home ownership
L. At the start of Scene 10 Blanche wears a white evening gown, slippers, and this.
M. Williams compares Blanche's manner and clothing to this.
N. He dumped Blanche when he found out about her past.
O. The name DuBois means this.
P. Game Stanley and the men played
Q. A woman's charm is fifty percent this.
R. Mitch's real name
S. Blanche depended on the kindness of ___.
T. He took his own life.
U. Meaning of Blanche's name
V. Blanche said he sent a telegram.
W. She accuses Steve of having an affair.
X. She ends up being sent to an institution.
Y. Stella calls Stanley a ___.

A Streetcar Named Desire Matching 2 Answer Key

U - 1. WHITE	A. Blanche says eating unwashed ___ will cause her to die.
X - 2. BLANCHE	B. Stanley smashed these on the wedding night.
A - 3. GRAPES	C. Blanche's sister; Stanley's wife
P - 4. POKER	D. Blanche physically threatens Stanley with a broken one.
C - 5. STELLA	E. Stella and Blanche are referred to as a pair of ___.
N - 6. MITCH	F. New Orleans
O - 7. WOOD	G. Blanche's astrological sign
R - 8. HAROLD	H. Blanche hears this, which is not actually playing.
M - 9. MOTH	I. It is named Desire.
Q -10. ILLUSION	J. Blanche's destination
L -11. TIARA	K. Proves home ownership
G -12. VIRGO	L. At the start of Scene 10 Blanche wears a white evening gown, slippers, and this.
S -13. STRANGERS	M. Williams compares Blanche's manner and clothing to this.
B -14. LIGHTBULBS	N. He dumped Blanche when he found out about her past.
F -15. SETTING	O. The name DuBois means this.
J -16. ASYLUM	P. Game Stanley and the men played
V -17. SHEP	Q. A woman's charm is fifty percent this.
I -18. STREETCAR	R. Mitch's real name
E -19. QUEENS	S. Blanche depended on the kindness of ___.
K -20. DEED	T. He took his own life.
Y -21. PIG	U. Meaning of Blanche's name
D -22. BOTTLE	V. Blanche said he sent a telegram.
T -23. ALLAN	W. She accuses Steve of having an affair.
W -24. EUNICE	X. She ends up being sent to an institution.
H -25. MUSIC	Y. Stella calls Stanley a ___.

A Streetcar Named Desire Matching 3

___ 1. HAROLD   A. Blanche's astrological sign
___ 2. FLAMINGO   B. He rapes Blanche.
___ 3. LIGHTBULBS   C. Blanche says only he could describe the Kowalskis' living conditions.
___ 4. VIRGO   D. Blanche says eating unwashed ___ will cause her to die.
___ 5. TICKET   E. In Stanley's joke, the rooster stopped pursuing the hen because of this.
___ 6. FIRE   F. Stella and Blanche are referred to as a pair of ___.
___ 7. POKER   G. Mitch's real name
___ 8. LEAVING   H. It would make Blanche weep with joy.
___ 9. STELLA   I. Stanley smashed these on the wedding night.
___10. DEED   J. Proves home ownership
___11. STANLEY   K. Cheap hotel of ill repute from which Blanche was asked to leave
___12. PREGNANT   L. According to Stella, this is Blanche's weakness.
___13. POE   M. She accuses Steve of having an affair.
___14. SILK   N. Meaning of Blanche's name
___15. GRAPES   O. Game Stanley and the men played
___16. ALLAN   P. He took his own life.
___17. MOTH   Q. The word Blanche screams
___18. CORN   R. Blanche's destination
___19. APPEARANCE   S. Williams compares Blanche's manner and clothing to this.
___20. ILLUSION   T. A woman's charm is fifty percent this.
___21. MUSIC   U. Blanche hears this, which is not actually playing.
___22. WHITE   V. Wedding night pajamas were made of this
___23. QUEENS   W. Blanche's sister; Stanley's wife
___24. EUNICE   X. Stella's condition
___25. ASYLUM   Y. Stanley buys Blanche one for her birthday.

A Streetcar Named Desire Matching 3 Answer Key

G - 1.	HAROLD	A. Blanche's astrological sign
K - 2.	FLAMINGO	B. He rapes Blanche.
I - 3.	LIGHTBULBS	C. Blanche says only he could describe the Kowalskis' living conditions.
A - 4.	VIRGO	D. Blanche says eating unwashed ___ will cause her to die.
Y - 5.	TICKET	E. In Stanley's joke, the rooster stopped pursuing the hen because of this.
Q - 6.	FIRE	F. Stella and Blanche are referred to as a pair of ___.
O - 7.	POKER	G. Mitch's real name
H - 8.	LEAVING	H. It would make Blanche weep with joy.
W - 9.	STELLA	I. Stanley smashed these on the wedding night.
J - 10.	DEED	J. Proves home ownership
B - 11.	STANLEY	K. Cheap hotel of ill repute from which Blanche was asked to leave
X - 12.	PREGNANT	L. According to Stella, this is Blanche's weakness.
C - 13.	POE	M. She accuses Steve of having an affair.
V - 14.	SILK	N. Meaning of Blanche's name
D - 15.	GRAPES	O. Game Stanley and the men played
P - 16.	ALLAN	P. He took his own life.
S - 17.	MOTH	Q. The word Blanche screams
E - 18.	CORN	R. Blanche's destination
L - 19.	APPEARANCE	S. Williams compares Blanche's manner and clothing to this.
T - 20.	ILLUSION	T. A woman's charm is fifty percent this.
U - 21.	MUSIC	U. Blanche hears this, which is not actually playing.
N - 22.	WHITE	V. Wedding night pajamas were made of this
F - 23.	QUEENS	W. Blanche's sister; Stanley's wife
M - 24.	EUNICE	X. Stella's condition
R - 25.	ASYLUM	Y. Stanley buys Blanche one for her birthday.

A Streetcar Named Desire Matching 4

___ 1. BOTTLE
___ 2. SETTING
___ 3. ALLAN
___ 4. RHINESTONES
___ 5. WILLIAMS
___ 6. FIRE
___ 7. CIGARETTE
___ 8. LANTERN
___ 9. POLISH
___10. VIRGO
___11. SHEP
___12. HAROLD
___13. STRANGERS
___14. MITCH
___15. TIARA
___16. BELLE
___17. LIGHTBULBS
___18. STANLEY
___19. WHITE
___20. MOTH
___21. WOOD
___22. STREETCAR
___23. FLAMINGO
___24. FLOWERS
___25. BLANCHE

A. Blanche said he sent a telegram.
B. Blanche depended on the kindness of ___.
C. He dumped Blanche when he found out about her past.
D. Stanley smashed these on the wedding night.
E. Cheap hotel of ill repute from which Blanche was asked to leave
F. The Mexican woman sells these.
G. The word Blanche screams
H. Author
I. Williams compares Blanche's manner and clothing to this.
J. He rapes Blanche.
K. The name DuBois means this.
L. Mitch's real name
M. Stanley's ethnic heritage
N. Lost plantation: ___ Reve
O. Blanche physically threatens Stanley with a broken one.
P. Meaning of Blanche's name
Q. Mitch's ____ case was from a former girlfriend.
R. Stanley asks Blanche if she wants to take her paper one with her.
S. New Orleans
T. It is named Desire.
U. She ends up being sent to an institution.
V. At the start of Scene 10 Blanche wears a white evening gown, slippers, and this.
W. False gems
X. Blanche's astrological sign
Y. He took his own life.

A Streetcar Named Desire Matching 4 Answer Key

O - 1. BOTTLE	A. Blanche said he sent a telegram.
S - 2. SETTING	B. Blanche depended on the kindness of ___.
Y - 3. ALLAN	C. He dumped Blanche when he found out about her past.
W - 4. RHINESTONES	D. Stanley smashed these on the wedding night.
H - 5. WILLIAMS	E. Cheap hotel of ill repute from which Blanche was asked to leave
G - 6. FIRE	F. The Mexican woman sells these.
Q - 7. CIGARETTE	G. The word Blanche screams
R - 8. LANTERN	H. Author
M - 9. POLISH	I. Williams compares Blanche's manner and clothing to this.
X - 10. VIRGO	J. He rapes Blanche.
A - 11. SHEP	K. The name DuBois means this.
L - 12. HAROLD	L. Mitch's real name
B - 13. STRANGERS	M. Stanley's ethnic heritage
C - 14. MITCH	N. Lost plantation: ___ Reve
V - 15. TIARA	O. Blanche physically threatens Stanley with a broken one.
N - 16. BELLE	P. Meaning of Blanche's name
D - 17. LIGHTBULBS	Q. Mitch's ___ case was from a former girlfriend.
J - 18. STANLEY	R. Stanley asks Blanche if she wants to take her paper one with her.
P - 19. WHITE	S. New Orleans
I - 20. MOTH	T. It is named Desire.
K - 21. WOOD	U. She ends up being sent to an institution.
T - 22. STREETCAR	V. At the start of Scene 10 Blanche wears a white evening gown, slippers, and this.
E - 23. FLAMINGO	W. False gems
F - 24. FLOWERS	X. Blanche's astrological sign
U - 25. BLANCHE	Y. He took his own life.

A Streetcar Named Desire Magic Squares 1

Match the definition with the vocabulary word. Put your answers in the magic squares below. When your answers are correct, all columns and rows will add to the same number.

A. LIFE
B. TICKET
C. STELLA
D. MUSIC
E. ELYSIAN
F. EUNICE
G. LEAVING
H. QUEENS
I. DEED
J. PIG
K. HAROLD
L. STRANGERS
M. ARMS
N. WOOD
O. LIGHTBULBS
P. MITCH

1. Blanche renames the Flamingo The Tarantula ___ Hotel.
2. She accuses Steve of having an affair.
3. Stella and Blanche are referred to as a pair of ___.
4. Stanley smashed these on the wedding night.
5. Blanche depended on the kindness of ___.
6. Blanche's sister; Stanley's wife
7. According to Eunice, it keeps on going.
8. Stella calls Stanley a ___.
9. Mitch's real name
10. Blanche hears this, which is not actually playing.
11. Stanley buys Blanche one for her birthday.
12. Proves home ownership
13. The name DuBois means this.
14. Ironic apartment name; ___ Fields
15. It would make Blanche weep with joy.
16. He dumped Blanche when he found out about her past.

A=	B=	C=	D=
E=	F=	G=	H=
I=	J=	K=	L=
M=	N=	O=	P=

A Streetcar Named Desire Magic Squares 1 Answer Key

Match the definition with the vocabulary word. Put your answers in the magic squares below. When your answers are correct, all columns and rows will add to the same number.

A. LIFE
B. TICKET
C. STELLA
D. MUSIC
E. ELYSIAN
F. EUNICE
G. LEAVING
H. QUEENS
I. DEED
J. PIG
K. HAROLD
L. STRANGERS
M. ARMS
N. WOOD
O. LIGHTBULBS
P. MITCH

1. Blanche renames the Flamingo The Tarantula ___ Hotel.
2. She accuses Steve of having an affair.
3. Stella and Blanche are referred to as a pair of ___.
4. Stanley smashed these on the wedding night.
5. Blanche depended on the kindness of ___.
6. Blanche's sister; Stanley's wife
7. According to Eunice, it keeps on going.
8. Stella calls Stanley a ___.
9. Mitch's real name
10. Blanche hears this, which is not actually playing.
11. Stanley buys Blanche one for her birthday.
12. Proves home ownership
13. The name DuBois means this.
14. Ironic apartment name; ___ Fields
15. It would make Blanche weep with joy.
16. He dumped Blanche when he found out about her past.

A=7	B=11	C=6	D=10
E=14	F=2	G=15	H=3
I=12	J=8	K=9	L=5
M=1	N=13	O=4	P=16

A Streetcar Named Desire Magic Squares 2

Match the definition with the vocabulary word. Put your answers in the magic squares below. When your answers are correct, all columns and rows will add to the same number.

A. FLAMINGO
B. LIGHTBULBS
C. POLISH
D. HOSPITAL
E. ASYLUM
F. LANTERN
G. TICKET
H. PIG
I. FLOWERS
J. ILLUSION
K. MUSIC
L. GRAPES
M. ARMS
N. STELLA
O. PLEIADES
P. BOTTLE

1. Stella calls Stanley a ___.
2. Cheap hotel of ill repute from which Blanche was asked to leave
3. Stanley smashed these on the wedding night.
4. Stanley buys Blanche one for her birthday.
5. A woman's charm is fifty percent this.
6. Blanche seeks this in the sky.
7. Blanche physically threatens Stanley with a broken one.
8. The Mexican woman sells these.
9. Blanche hears this, which is not actually playing.
10. Blanche's sister; Stanley's wife
11. Blanche renames the Flamingo The Tarantula ___ Hotel.
12. Blanche says eating unwashed ___ will cause her to die.
13. Blanche's destination
14. Stella is rushed there.
15. Stanley's ethnic heritage
16. Stanley asks Blanche if she wants to take her paper one with her.

A=	B=	C=	D=
E=	F=	G=	H=
I=	J=	K=	L=
M=	N=	O=	P=

A Streetcar Named Desire Magic Squares 2 Answer Key

Match the definition with the vocabulary word. Put your answers in the magic squares below. When your answers are correct, all columns and rows will add to the same number.

A. FLAMINGO
B. LIGHTBULBS
C. POLISH
D. HOSPITAL
E. ASYLUM
F. LANTERN
G. TICKET
H. PIG
I. FLOWERS
J. ILLUSION
K. MUSIC
L. GRAPES
M. ARMS
N. STELLA
O. PLEIADES
P. BOTTLE

1. Stella calls Stanley a ___.
2. Cheap hotel of ill repute from which Blanche was asked to leave
3. Stanley smashed these on the wedding night.
4. Stanley buys Blanche one for her birthday.
5. A woman's charm is fifty percent this.
6. Blanche seeks this in the sky.
7. Blanche physically threatens Stanley with a broken one.
8. The Mexican woman sells these.
9. Blanche hears this, which is not actually playing.
10. Blanche's sister; Stanley's wife
11. Blanche renames the Flamingo The Tarantula ___ Hotel.
12. Blanche says eating unwashed ___ will cause her to die.
13. Blanche's destination
14. Stella is rushed there.
15. Stanley's ethnic heritage
16. Stanley asks Blanche if she wants to take her paper one with her.

A=2	B=3	C=15	D=14
E=13	F=16	G=4	H=1
I=8	J=5	K=9	L=12
M=11	N=10	O=6	P=7

A Streetcar Named Desire Magic Squares 3

Match the definition with the vocabulary word. Put your answers in the magic squares below. When your answers are correct, all columns and rows will add to the same number.

A. BOTTLE
B. TICKET
C. PIG
D. MOTH
E. FLAMINGO
F. LIGHTBULBS
G. BUTTONS
H. EUNICE
I. MUSIC
J. MITCH
K. STREETCAR
L. FLOWERS
M. PLEIADES
N. STRANGERS
O. VIRGO
P. ILLUSION

1. Stella calls Stanley a ___.
2. He dumped Blanche when he found out about her past.
3. Stanley smashed these on the wedding night.
4. Blanche's astrological sign
5. A woman's charm is fifty percent this.
6. Cheap hotel of ill repute from which Blanche was asked to leave
7. Blanche hears this, which is not actually playing.
8. Williams compares Blanche's manner and clothing to this.
9. Blanche seeks this in the sky.
10. She accuses Steve of having an affair.
11. The Mexican woman sells these.
12. Blanche physically threatens Stanley with a broken one.
13. Stanley buys Blanche one for her birthday.
14. It is named Desire.
15. Blanche asks Stanley for help with these.
16. Blanche depended on the kindness of ___.

A=	B=	C=	D=
E=	F=	G=	H=
I=	J=	K=	L=
M=	N=	O=	P=

A Streetcar Named Desire Magic Squares 3 Answer Key

Match the definition with the vocabulary word. Put your answers in the magic squares below. When your answers are correct, all columns and rows will add to the same number.

A. BOTTLE
B. TICKET
C. PIG
D. MOTH
E. FLAMINGO
F. LIGHTBULBS
G. BUTTONS
H. EUNICE
I. MUSIC
J. MITCH
K. STREETCAR
L. FLOWERS
M. PLEIADES
N. STRANGERS
O. VIRGO
P. ILLUSION

1. Stella calls Stanley a ___.
2. He dumped Blanche when he found out about her past.
3. Stanley smashed these on the wedding night.
4. Blanche's astrological sign
5. A woman's charm is fifty percent this.
6. Cheap hotel of ill repute from which Blanche was asked to leave
7. Blanche hears this, which is not actually playing.
8. Williams compares Blanche's manner and clothing to this.
9. Blanche seeks this in the sky.
10. She accuses Steve of having an affair.
11. The Mexican woman sells these.
12. Blanche physically threatens Stanley with a broken one.
13. Stanley buys Blanche one for her birthday.
14. It is named Desire.
15. Blanche asks Stanley for help with these.
16. Blanche depended on the kindness of ___.

A=12	B=13	C=1	D=8
E=6	F=3	G=15	H=10
I=7	J=2	K=14	L=11
M=9	N=16	O=4	P=5

A Streetcar Named Desire Magic Squares 4

Match the definition with the vocabulary word. Put your answers in the magic squares below. When your answers are correct, all columns and rows will add to the same number.

A. POKER
B. WILLIAMS
C. HOSPITAL
D. SHEP
E. VIRGO
F. STRANGERS
G. PREGNANT
H. TICKET
I. TIARA
J. MOTH
K. ASYLUM
L. SETTING
M. ELYSIAN
N. WOOD
O. RADIO
P. LEAVING

1. Game Stanley and the men played
2. The name DuBois means this.
3. Williams compares Blanche's manner and clothing to this.
4. Blanche's astrological sign
5. Stella's condition
6. New Orleans
7. It would make Blanche weep with joy.
8. Stella is rushed there.
9. Stanley threw it out the window.
10. Blanche said he sent a telegram.
11. Stanley buys Blanche one for her birthday.
12. Blanche's destination
13. At the start of Scene 10 Blanche wears a white evening gown, slippers, and this.
14. Blanche depended on the kindness of ___.
15. Author
16. Ironic apartment name; ___ Fields

A=	B=	C=	D=
E=	F=	G=	H=
I=	J=	K=	L=
M=	N=	O=	P=

A Streetcar Named Desire Magic Squares 4 Answer Key

Match the definition with the vocabulary word. Put your answers in the magic squares below. When your answers are correct, all columns and rows will add to the same number.

A. POKER
B. WILLIAMS
C. HOSPITAL
D. SHEP
E. VIRGO
F. STRANGERS
G. PREGNANT
H. TICKET
I. TIARA
J. MOTH
K. ASYLUM
L. SETTING
M. ELYSIAN
N. WOOD
O. RADIO
P. LEAVING

1. Game Stanley and the men played
2. The name DuBois means this.
3. Williams compares Blanche's manner and clothing to this.
4. Blanche's astrological sign
5. Stella's condition
6. New Orleans
7. It would make Blanche weep with joy.
8. Stella is rushed there.
9. Stanley threw it out the window.
10. Blanche said he sent a telegram.
11. Stanley buys Blanche one for her birthday.
12. Blanche's destination
13. At the start of Scene 10 Blanche wears a white evening gown, slippers, and this.
14. Blanche depended on the kindness of ___.
15. Author
16. Ironic apartment name; ___ Fields

A=1	B=15	C=8	D=10
E=4	F=14	G=5	H=11
I=13	J=3	K=12	L=6
M=16	N=2	O=9	P=7

A Streetcar Named Desire Word Search 1

```
F L A M I N G O E L Y S I A N C O D E C
L L S F P L G H T Q Q W X L Z S O L U T
O H T O M R F G I S U P I V L O X M N D
W R R Z I B K M H Z F E J L W U R V I S
E S A V Q A A B W P O K E R L C S X C S
R N N D L T W L L Z N T D N M I B I E H
S O G L I S I R L A H E V I S G A P O W
P T E H G O T A X A N K T P B A A M W N
H T R A P P E A R A N C E C O R N A S W
S U S G E F O O N A H I H L G E L R I B
H B B H I X L L M L R T E E E T A M L B
A P S L D D E U I B E L L E M T N S K N
W V I E G R L G W S R Y T T U E T L L Q
G L E G I Y X W F K H S T Q S W E E S P
Z D N F S C L A T I P S O H I N R Z R R
L V X A L I G H T B U L B S C M N W P S
```

A woman's charm is fifty percent this. (8)
According to Eunice, it keeps on going. (4)
According to Stella, this is Blanche's weakness. (10)
At the start of Scene 10 Blanche wears a white evening gown, slippers, and this. (5)
Author (8)
Blanche asks Stanley for help with these. (7)
Blanche depended on the kindness of ___. (9)
Blanche hears this, which is not actually playing. (5)
Blanche physically threatens Stanley with a broken one. (6)
Blanche renames the Flamingo The Tarantula ___ Hotel. (4)
Blanche said he sent a telegram. (4)
Blanche says eating unwashed ___ will cause her to die. (6)
Blanche says only he could describe the Kowalskis' living conditions. (3)
Blanche says she'll burn these that Stanley has touched. (7)
Blanche's astrological sign (5)
Blanche's destination (6)
Blanche's sister; Stanley's wife (6)
Cheap hotel of ill repute from which Blanche was asked to leave (8)
Game Stanley and the men played (5)
He dumped Blanche when he found out about her past. (5)
He knows the gossip about Blanche. (4)
He rapes Blanche. (7)

He took his own life. (5)
In Stanley's joke, the rooster stopped pursuing the hen because of this. (4)
Ironic apartment name; ___ Fields (7)
Lost plantation: ___ Reve (5)
Meaning of Blanche's name (5)
Mitch's ____ case was from a former girlfriend. (9)
Mitch's real name (6)
Proves home ownership (4)
She accuses Steve of having an affair. (6)
She ends up being sent to an institution. (7)
Stanley asks Blanche if she wants to take her paper one with her. (7)
Stanley buys Blanche one for her birthday. (6)
Stanley says spousal ownership of property is the Napoleonic ___. (4)
Stanley smashed these on the wedding night. (10)
Stanley threw it out the window. (5)
Stanley's ethnic heritage (6)
Stella and Blanche are referred to as a pair of ___. (6)
Stella calls Stanley a ___. (3)
Stella is rushed there. (8)
The Mexican woman sells these. (7)
The name DuBois means this. (4)
The word Blanche screams (4)
Wedding night pajamas were made of this (4)
Williams compares Blanche's manner and clothing to this. (4)

A Streetcar Named Desire Word Search 1 Answer Key

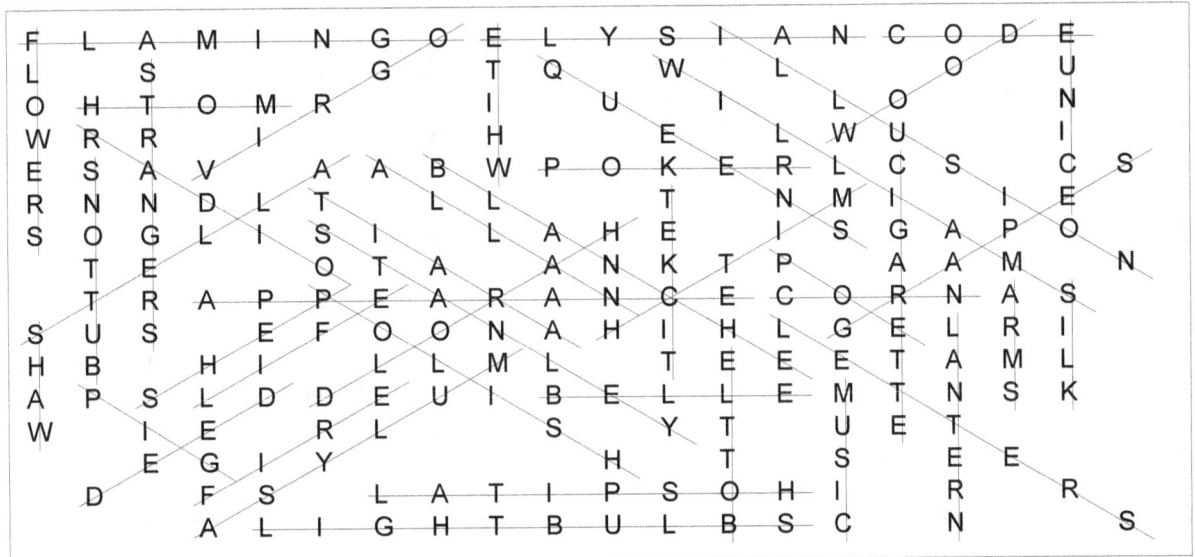

A woman's charm is fifty percent this. (8)
According to Eunice, it keeps on going. (4)
According to Stella, this is Blanche's weakness. (10)
At the start of Scene 10 Blanche wears a white evening gown, slippers, and this. (5)
Author (8)
Blanche asks Stanley for help with these. (7)
Blanche depended on the kindness of ___. (9)
Blanche hears this, which is not actually playing. (5)
Blanche physically threatens Stanley with a broken one. (6)
Blanche renames the Flamingo The Tarantula ___ Hotel. (4)
Blanche said he sent a telegram. (4)
Blanche says eating unwashed ___ will cause her to die. (6)
Blanche says only he could describe the Kowalskis' living conditions. (3)
Blanche says she'll burn these that Stanley has touched. (7)
Blanche's astrological sign (5)
Blanche's destination (6)
Blanche's sister; Stanley's wife (6)
Cheap hotel of ill repute from which Blanche was asked to leave (8)
Game Stanley and the men played (5)
He dumped Blanche when he found out about her past. (5)
He knows the gossip about Blanche. (4)
He rapes Blanche. (7)

He took his own life. (5)
In Stanley's joke, the rooster stopped pursuing the hen because of this. (4)
Ironic apartment name; ___ Fields (7)
Lost plantation: ___ Reve (5)
Meaning of Blanche's name (5)
Mitch's ___ case was from a former girlfriend. (9)
Mitch's real name (6)
Proves home ownership (4)
She accuses Steve of having an affair. (6)
She ends up being sent to an institution. (7)
Stanley asks Blanche if she wants to take her paper one with her. (7)
Stanley buys Blanche one for her birthday. (6)
Stanley says spousal ownership of property is the Napoleonic ___. (4)
Stanley smashed these on the wedding night. (10)
Stanley threw it out the window. (5)
Stanley's ethnic heritage (6)
Stella and Blanche are referred to as a pair of ___. (6)
Stella calls Stanley a ___. (3)
Stella is rushed there. (8)
The Mexican woman sells these. (7)
The name DuBois means this. (4)
The word Blanche screams (4)
Wedding night pajamas were made of this (4)
Williams compares Blanche's manner and clothing to this. (4)

A Streetcar Named Desire Word Search 2

A	P	P	E	A	R	A	N	C	E	T	F	B	V	S	T	E	L	L	A
R	G	R	A	P	E	S	O	B	W	A	I	J	G	H	D	H	S	B	P
A	E	U	N	I	C	E	I	Y	L	O	S	C	V	A	E	N	V	N	N
I	F	L	O	W	E	R	S	T	D	A	O	Y	K	W	E	F	I	N	S
T	Z	K	T	C	S	S	U	Y	L	M	N	D	L	E	D	T	R	R	B
R	S	E	D	A	I	E	L	P	O	S	Q	C	U	U	T	C	G	E	S
A	B	R	S	Y	Z	T	L	D	R	Q	S	Q	H	L	M	K	O	T	R
D	L	P	Y	T	C	T	I	E	A	R	W	S	Q	E	I	H	P	N	Z
I	U	M	T	K	A	I	G	Q	H	I	I	G	N	T	S	F	O	A	F
O	B	A	L	L	A	N	B	E	L	L	E	G	N	I	V	A	E	L	W
A	T	D	M	W	A	G	L	L	K	M	X	A	L	H	Z	Q	A	H	N
R	H	Z	O	R	G	K	I	E	R	Y	N	O	Z	W	M	M	R	C	F
M	G	K	T	F	W	A	M	E	Y	G	P	P	E	R	I	F	X	T	F
S	I	S	H	C	M	T	K	L	E	V	E	Z	Q	N	M	U	S	I	C
M	L	X	J	S	X	O	L	R	P	H	B	X	G	C	O	R	N	M	R
T	P	I	G	R	P	D	P	Z	S	H	B	O	T	T	L	E	D	O	C

A woman's charm is fifty percent this. (8)
According to Eunice, it keeps on going. (4)
According to Stella, this is Blanche's weakness. (10)
At the start of Scene 10 Blanche wears a white evening gown, slippers, and this. (5)
Author (8)
Blanche depended on the kindness of ___. (9)
Blanche hears this, which is not actually playing. (5)
Blanche physically threatens Stanley with a broken one. (6)
Blanche renames the Flamingo The Tarantula ___ Hotel. (4)
Blanche said he sent a telegram. (4)
Blanche says eating unwashed ___ will cause her to die. (6)
Blanche says only he could describe the Kowalskis' living conditions. (3)
Blanche seeks this in the sky. (8)
Blanche's astrological sign (5)
Blanche's destination (6)
Blanche's sister; Stanley's wife (6)
Cheap hotel of ill repute from which Blanche was asked to leave (8)
Game Stanley and the men played (5)
He dumped Blanche when he found out about her past. (5)
He knows the gossip about Blanche. (4)
He rapes Blanche. (7)
He took his own life. (5)
In Stanley's joke, the rooster stopped pursuing the hen because of this. (4)
It would make Blanche weep with joy. (7)
Lost plantation: ___ Reve (5)
Meaning of Blanche's name (5)
Mitch's real name (6)
New Orleans (7)
Proves home ownership (4)
She accuses Steve of having an affair. (6)
She ends up being sent to an institution. (7)
Stanley asks Blanche if she wants to take her paper one with her. (7)
Stanley buys Blanche one for her birthday. (6)
Stanley says spousal ownership of property is the Napoleonic ___. (4)
Stanley smashed these on the wedding night. (10)
Stanley threw it out the window. (5)
Stanley's ethnic heritage (6)
Stella and Blanche are referred to as a pair of ___. (6)
Stella calls Stanley a ___. (3)
Stella's condition (8)
The Mexican woman sells these. (7)
The name DuBois means this. (4)
The word Blanche screams (4)
Wedding night pajamas were made of this (4)
Williams compares Blanche's manner and clothing to this. (4)

A Streetcar Named Desire Word Search 2 Answer Key

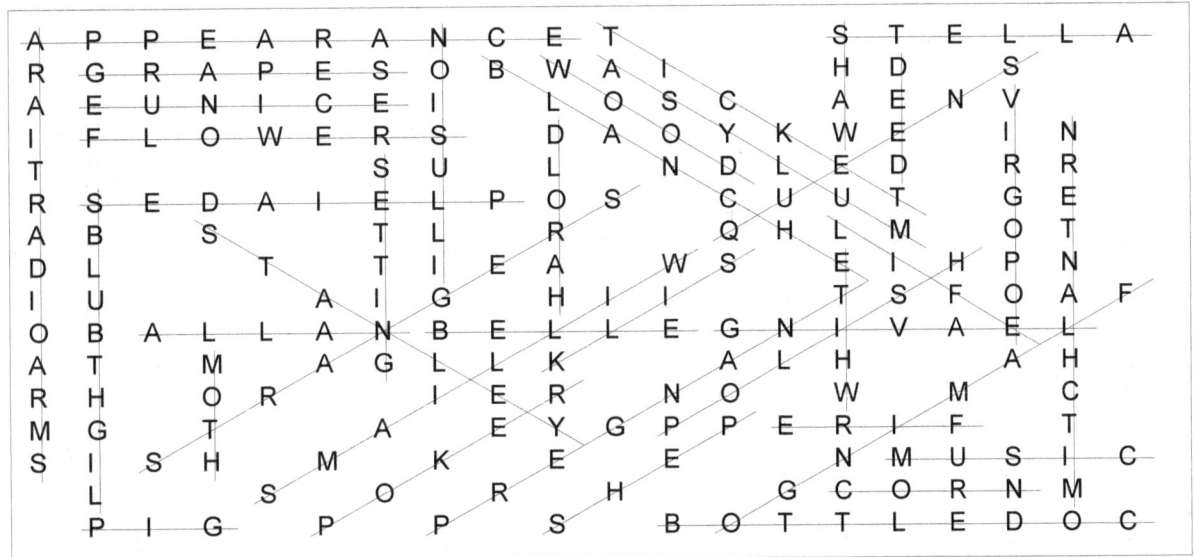

A woman's charm is fifty percent this. (8)
According to Eunice, it keeps on going. (4)
According to Stella, this is Blanche's weakness. (10)
At the start of Scene 10 Blanche wears a white evening gown, slippers, and this. (5)
Author (8)
Blanche depended on the kindness of ___. (9)
Blanche hears this, which is not actually playing. (5)
Blanche physically threatens Stanley with a broken one. (6)
Blanche renames the Flamingo The Tarantula ___ Hotel. (4)
Blanche said he sent a telegram. (4)
Blanche says eating unwashed ___ will cause her to die. (6)
Blanche says only he could describe the Kowalskis' living conditions. (3)
Blanche seeks this in the sky. (8)
Blanche's astrological sign (5)
Blanche's destination (6)
Blanche's sister; Stanley's wife (6)
Cheap hotel of ill repute from which Blanche was asked to leave (8)
Game Stanley and the men played (5)
He dumped Blanche when he found out about her past. (5)
He knows the gossip about Blanche. (4)
He rapes Blanche. (7)
He took his own life. (5)
In Stanley's joke, the rooster stopped pursuing the hen because of this. (4)
It would make Blanche weep with joy. (7)
Lost plantation: ___ Reve (5)
Meaning of Blanche's name (5)
Mitch's real name (6)
New Orleans (7)
Proves home ownership (4)
She accuses Steve of having an affair. (6)
She ends up being sent to an institution. (7)
Stanley asks Blanche if she wants to take her paper one with her. (7)
Stanley buys Blanche one for her birthday. (6)
Stanley says spousal ownership of property is the Napoleonic ___. (4)
Stanley smashed these on the wedding night. (10)
Stanley threw it out the window. (5)
Stanley's ethnic heritage (6)
Stella and Blanche are referred to as a pair of ___. (6)
Stella calls Stanley a ___. (3)
Stella's condition (8)
The Mexican woman sells these. (7)
The name DuBois means this. (4)
The word Blanche screams (4)
Wedding night pajamas were made of this (4)
Williams compares Blanche's manner and clothing to this. (4)

A Streetcar Named Desire Word Search 3

```
B D F B M C M F L O W E R S P O L I S H
R C C I B N B R Z B Z S T A N L E Y S H W
N Z W L C W J V F X J P J K W L E K W J W Y
H V C L S W N H A F P F R Q F K S H L A Q
M G X U G R A P E S Q P O E L Y S I A N D
V S Y S R N E T H L Y R M R G F K T L L D
R L S I B H S E R E Q L N Z L N R E C K
D T A O C S P E H A M R U A G R A W K X
C O R N S N K W L V Y W M M R L S N S B
Y I A G T O T P S I W I O X I R G Z T N
S L G Q P E G D I N N W T G E M L S S M
B H R A K S R R Z G V N H T B X U S M J
A Z A H R T E N O P X T T L D O W S A P
L P C W J E Y T Z Z B E L W X V T B I P
L V T H M L T M T U L B E L L E A T L C
A C E O Z L S T L I Z I D S D F P X L M
N W E S Y A J B E B N O F R Q E P H I E
C S R P K F S S Y H O G P E V T E R W W
O G T I M A C M A W E F L G W I A D L Z
D S S T R M T R I C T I E N S C R Q N F
E X S A V N O A I T S R I A Q K A G P G
H L I L Q L J N C L C E A R R E N J O G
J T F M D Q U G H B R H D T J T C H Q F
P R H I N E S T O N E S E S D S E N V W
R A D I O B U T T O N S N E E U Q X D
```

ALLAN
APPEARANCE
ARMS
ASYLUM
BELLE
BLANCHE
BOTTLE
BUTTONS
CIGARETTE
CODE
CORN
DEED
ELYSIAN
EUNICE
FIRE
FLAMINGO
FLOWERS
GRAPES

HAROLD
HOSPITAL
ILLUSION
LANTERN
LEAVING
LETTERS
LIFE
LIGHTBULBS
MITCH
MOTH
MUSIC
PIG
PLEIADES
POE
POKER
POLISH
PREGNANT
QUEENS

RADIO
RHINESTONES
SETTING
SHAW
SHEP
SILK
STANLEY
STELLA
STRANGERS
STREETCAR
TIARA
TICKET
VIRGO
WHITE
WILLIAMS
WOOD

A Streetcar Named Desire Word Search 3 Answer Key

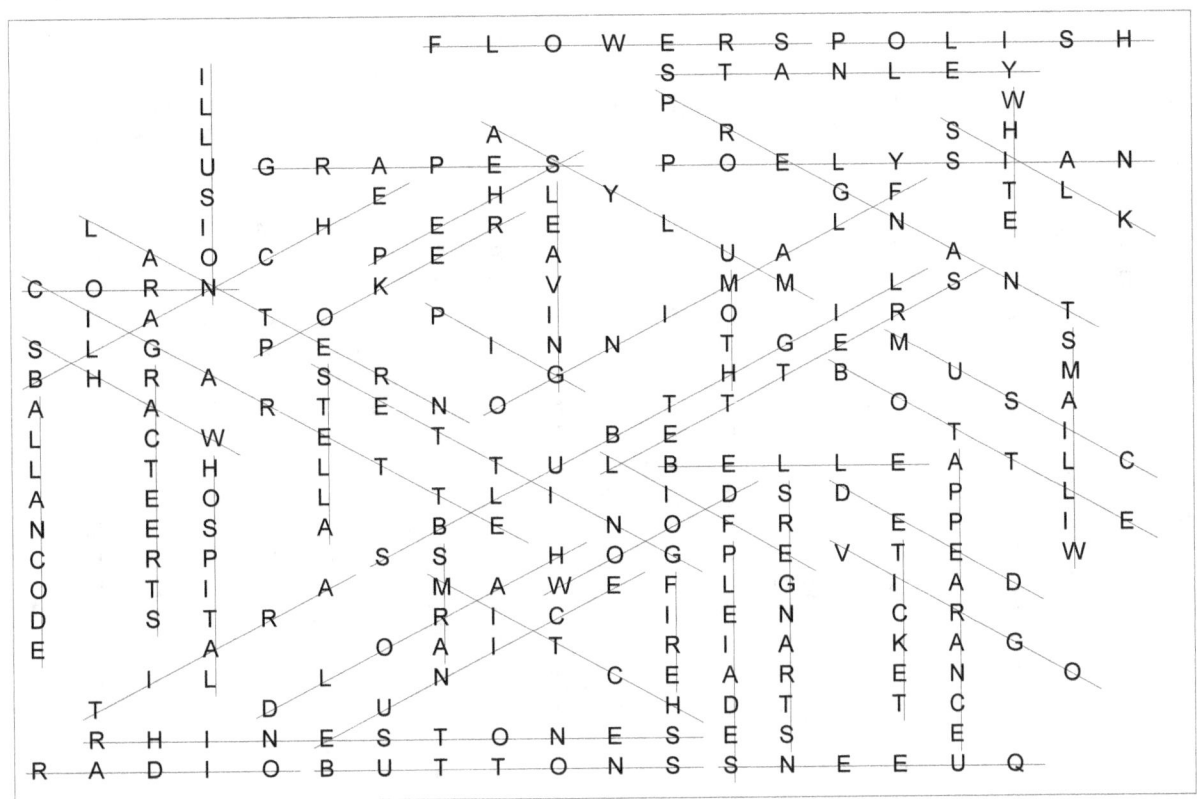

ALLAN	HAROLD	RADIO
APPEARANCE	HOSPITAL	RHINESTONES
ARMS	ILLUSION	SETTING
ASYLUM	LANTERN	SHAW
BELLE	LEAVING	SHEP
BLANCHE	LETTERS	SILK
BOTTLE	LIFE	STANLEY
BUTTONS	LIGHTBULBS	STELLA
CIGARETTE	MITCH	STRANGERS
CODE	MOTH	STREETCAR
CORN	MUSIC	TIARA
DEED	PIG	TICKET
ELYSIAN	PLEIADES	VIRGO
EUNICE	POE	WHITE
FIRE	POKER	WILLIAMS
FLAMINGO	POLISH	WOOD
FLOWERS	PREGNANT	
GRAPES	QUEENS	

A Streetcar Named Desire Word Search 4

```
S G X C B H A R O L D N P P B I T H R C
Y T Y I V U B T M V G M L N E L I C H M
W Y R G S X T W J K Z M E G L L A K I K
B G D A J T V T Z M G R I V L U R G N C
S S X R N W R M O D G T A X E S A R N K
J Z P E T G X E Y N S D N Y I X Y E L L
Y B F T Y F E B E N S D E J J O M Y S C
P P K T G Q G R Z T L W S D M N N W T F
F R R E S N F X S S C D V S N F R W O F
J M E Q V L R N N W A R T L K E S N E Q
Y C W G A C N M A H C R E A K T C S S D
P K O Z N S M M C L I R S L R W N I S W
M O N D L A I L O T T R Q L M D A S Q G
G G K H E C N A R A E P P A S Y L U M F
H R D E Y Z G T N W O L Z T V I E M O M
O A Q E R C O G O L V W Y F I E L S T M
S P B C E Z R L I B P G Y S N C B K H F
P E L R S D F S W Y O H S S I L K E M B
I S A E A M H W W I E T E H U A F E I V
T C N S A D B H P X L Q T B A I N H T C
A T C W H V I N I W D L T L W V H C Z F
L Z H L O E I O G S W H I K E R I F H F
N R E K H O P N C P G W N A P R G M K C
H F X N T C D L G I K Z G T M R G B C L
E U N I C E B W L E T T E R S S O L C T
```

ALLAN
APPEARANCE
ARMS
ASYLUM
BELLE
BLANCHE
BOTTLE
BUTTONS
CIGARETTE
CODE
CORN
DEED
ELYSIAN
EUNICE
FIRE
FLAMINGO
FLOWERS
GRAPES

HAROLD
HOSPITAL
ILLUSION
LANTERN
LEAVING
LETTERS
LIFE
LIGHTBULBS
MITCH
MOTH
MUSIC
PIG
PLEIADES
POE
POKER
POLISH
PREGNANT
QUEENS

RADIO
RHINESTONES
SETTING
SHAW
SHEP
SILK
STANLEY
STELLA
STRANGERS
STREETCAR
TIARA
TICKET
VIRGO
WHITE
WILLIAMS
WOOD

A Streetcar Named Desire Word Search 4 Answer Key

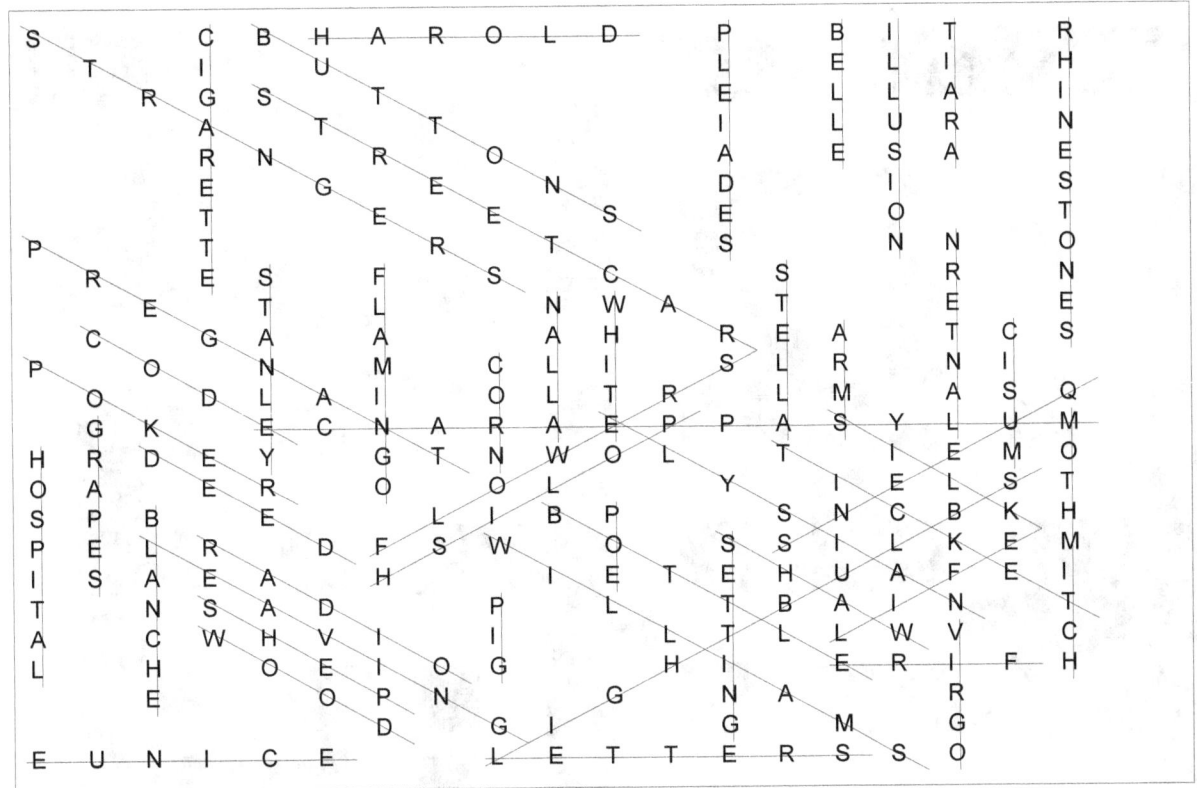

ALLAN	HAROLD	RADIO
APPEARANCE	HOSPITAL	RHINESTONES
ARMS	ILLUSION	SETTING
ASYLUM	LANTERN	SHAW
BELLE	LEAVING	SHEP
BLANCHE	LETTERS	SILK
BOTTLE	LIFE	STANLEY
BUTTONS	LIGHTBULBS	STELLA
CIGARETTE	MITCH	STRANGERS
CODE	MOTH	STREETCAR
CORN	MUSIC	TIARA
DEED	PIG	TICKET
ELYSIAN	PLEIADES	VIRGO
EUNICE	POE	WHITE
FIRE	POKER	WILLIAMS
FLAMINGO	POLISH	WOOD
FLOWERS	PREGNANT	
GRAPES	QUEENS	

A Streetcar Named Desire Crossword 1

Across
2. Stanley's ethnic heritage
5. Stella is rushed there.
7. He took his own life.
8. In Stanley's joke, the rooster stopped pursuing the hen because of this.
9. Stanley threw it out the window.
10. He knows the gossip about Blanche.
13. Proves home ownership
14. Blanche says only he could describe the Kowalskis' living conditions.
15. Blanche says eating unwashed ___ will cause her to die.
16. Blanche said he sent a telegram.
17. Blanche physically threatens Stanley with a broken one.
19. Cheap hotel of ill repute from which Blanche was asked to leave

Down
1. At the start of Scene 10 Blanche wears a white evening gown, slippers, and this.
2. Blanche seeks this in the sky.
3. It would make Blanche weep with joy.
4. Wedding night pajamas were made of this
5. Mitch's real name
6. He rapes Blanche.
10. Blanche's sister; Stanley's wife
11. Author
12. Stanley asks Blanche if she wants to take her paper one with her.
14. Stella's condition
17. Lost plantation: ___ Reve
18. Williams compares Blanche's manner and clothing to this.
19. The word Blanche screams
20. Blanche renames the Flamingo The Tarantula ___ Hotel.

A Streetcar Named Desire Crossword 1 Answer Key

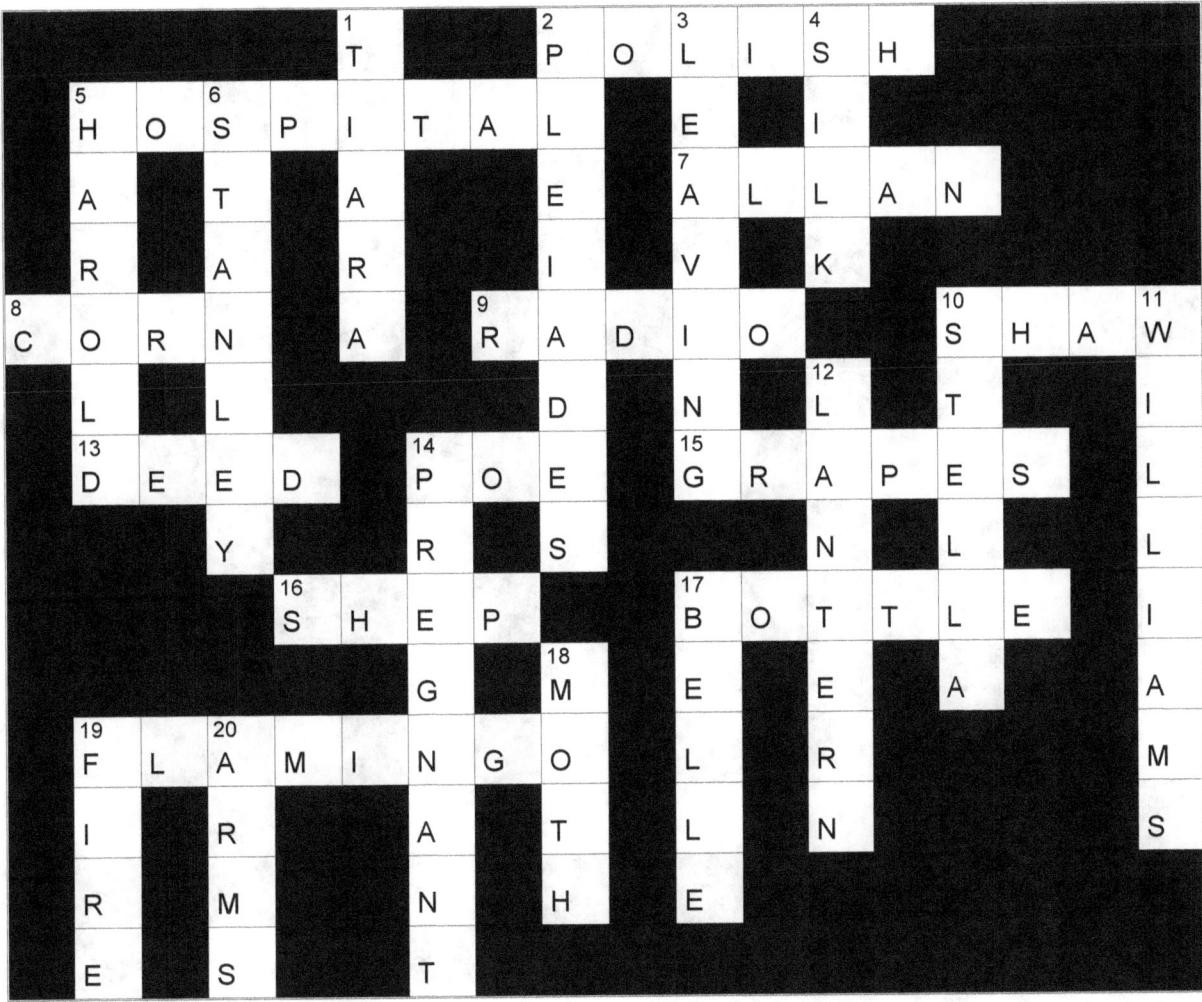

Across
2. Stanley's ethnic heritage
5. Stella is rushed there.
7. He took his own life.
8. In Stanley's joke, the rooster stopped pursuing the hen because of this.
9. Stanley threw it out the window.
10. He knows the gossip about Blanche.
13. Proves home ownership
14. Blanche says only he could describe the Kowalskis' living conditions.
15. Blanche says eating unwashed ___ will cause her to die.
16. Blanche said he sent a telegram.
17. Blanche physically threatens Stanley with a broken one.
19. Cheap hotel of ill repute from which Blanche was asked to leave

Down
1. At the start of Scene 10 Blanche wears a white evening gown, slippers, and this.
2. Blanche seeks this in the sky.
3. It would make Blanche weep with joy.
4. Wedding night pajamas were made of this
5. Mitch's real name
6. He rapes Blanche.
10. Blanche's sister; Stanley's wife
11. Author
12. Stanley asks Blanche if she wants to take her paper one with her.
14. Stella's condition
17. Lost plantation: ___ Reve
18. Williams compares Blanche's manner and clothing to this.
19. The word Blanche screams
20. Blanche renames the Flamingo The Tarantula ___ Hotel.

A Streetcar Named Desire Crossword 2

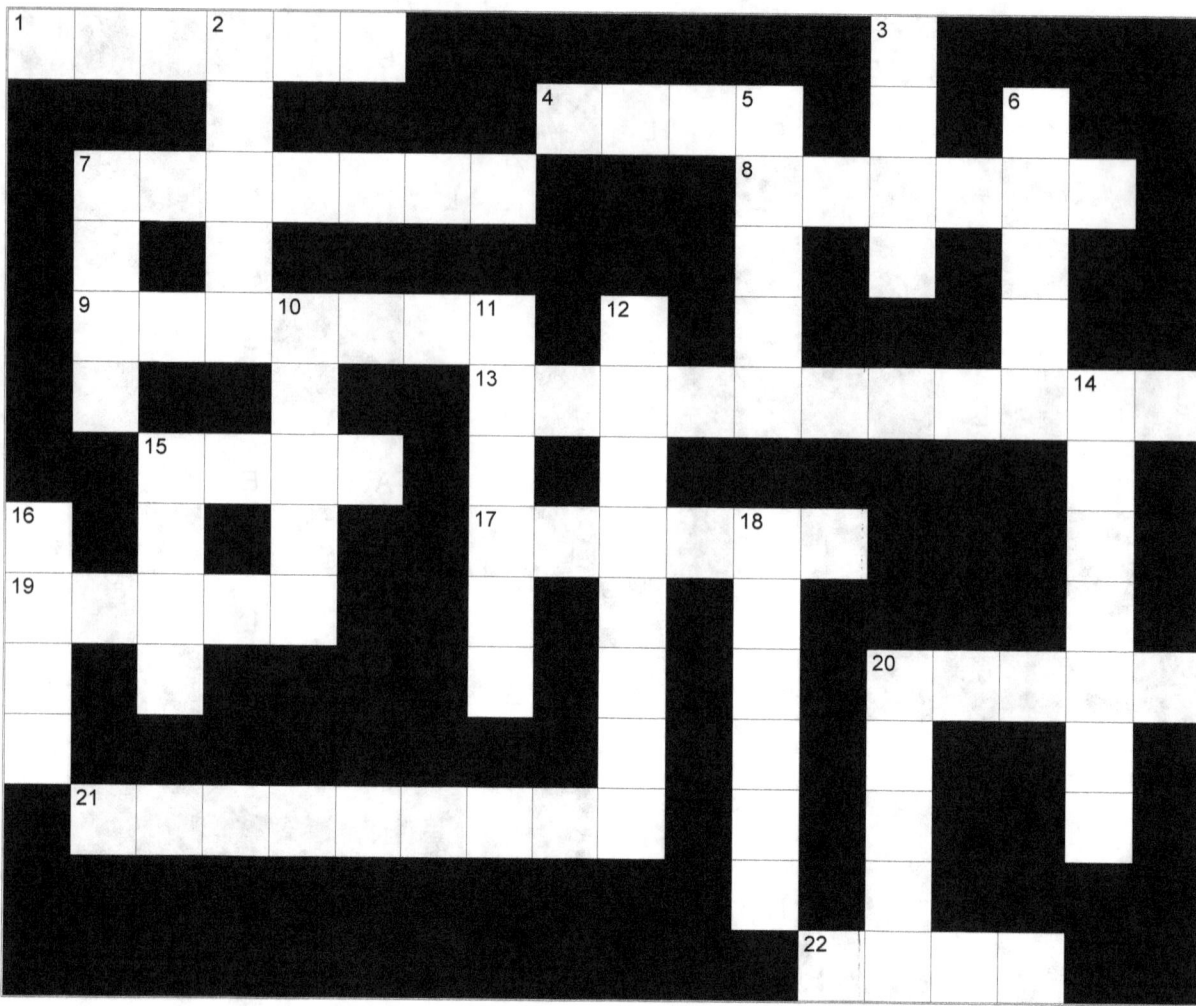

Across
1. Blanche physically threatens Stanley with a broken one.
4. He knows the gossip about Blanche.
7. He rapes Blanche.
8. Mitch's real name
9. It would make Blanche weep with joy.
13. False gems
15. In Stanley's joke, the rooster stopped pursuing the hen because of this.
17. Stanley's ethnic heritage
19. Stanley threw it out the window.
20. Blanche hears this, which is not actually playing.
21. Blanche depended on the kindness of ___.
22. Blanche said he sent a telegram.

Down
2. At the start of Scene 10 Blanche wears a white evening gown, slippers, and this.
3. The word Blanche screams
5. Meaning of Blanche's name
6. He took his own life.
7. Wedding night pajamas were made of this
10. Blanche's astrological sign
11. Blanche says eating unwashed ___ will cause her to die.
12. Author
14. Ironic apartment name; ___ Fields
15. Stanley says spousal ownership of property is the Napoleonic ___.
16. Blanche renames the Flamingo The Tarantula ___ Hotel.
18. Blanche's sister; Stanley's wife
20. He dumped Blanche when he found out about her past.

A Streetcar Named Desire Crossword 2 Answer Key

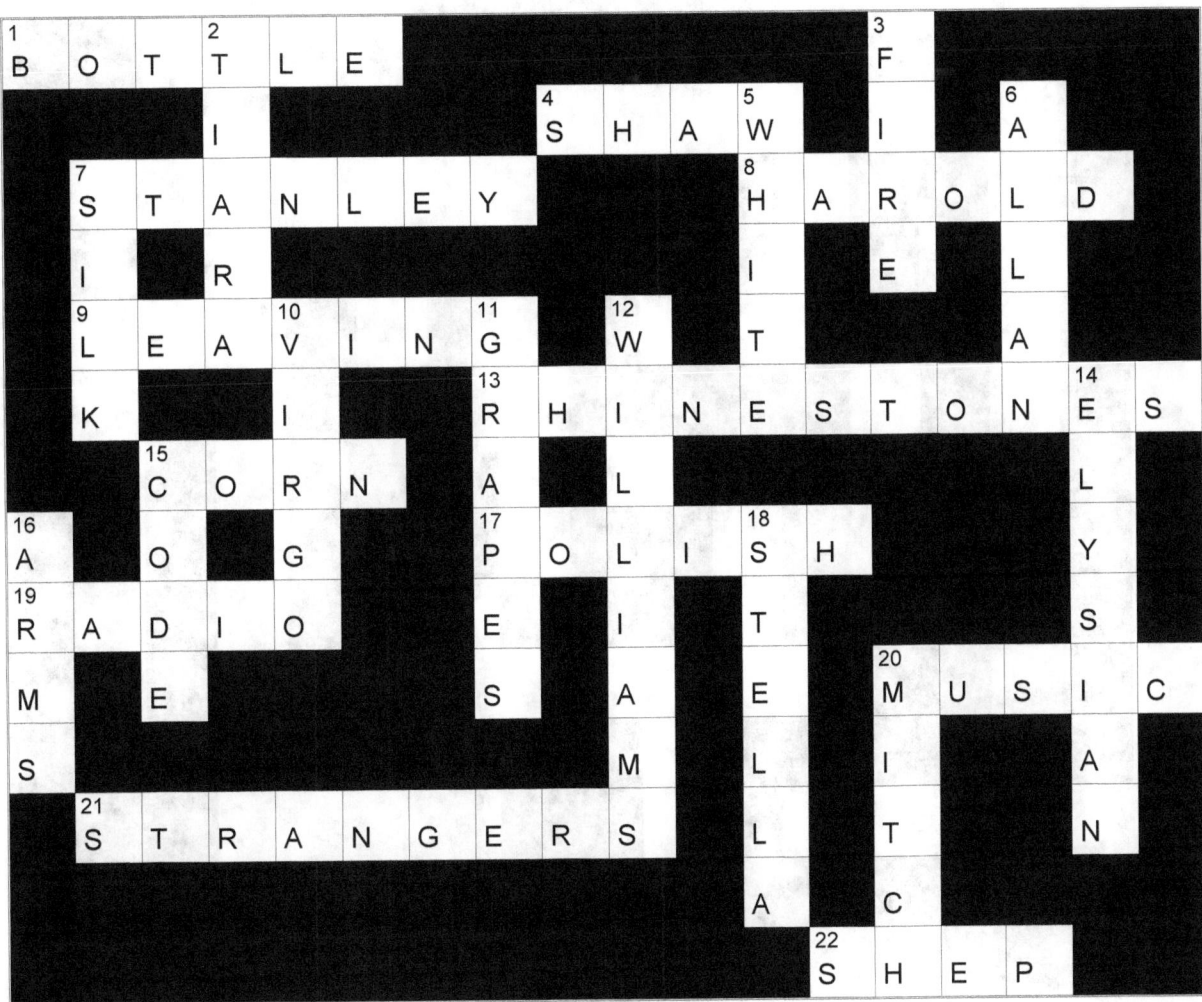

Across
1. Blanche physically threatens Stanley with a broken one.
4. He knows the gossip about Blanche.
7. He rapes Blanche.
8. Mitch's real name
9. It would make Blanche weep with joy.
13. False gems
15. In Stanley's joke, the rooster stopped pursuing the hen because of this.
17. Stanley's ethnic heritage
19. Stanley threw it out the window.
20. Blanche hears this, which is not actually playing.
21. Blanche depended on the kindness of ___.
22. Blanche said he sent a telegram.

Down
2. At the start of Scene 10 Blanche wears a white evening gown, slippers, and this.
3. The word Blanche screams
5. Meaning of Blanche's name
6. He took his own life.
7. Wedding night pajamas were made of this
10. Blanche's astrological sign
11. Blanche says eating unwashed ___ will cause her to die.
12. Author
14. Ironic apartment name; ___ Fields
15. Stanley says spousal ownership of property is the Napoleonic ___.
16. Blanche renames the Flamingo The Tarantula ___ Hotel.
18. Blanche's sister; Stanley's wife
20. He dumped Blanche when he found out about her past.

A Streetcar Named Desire Crossword 3

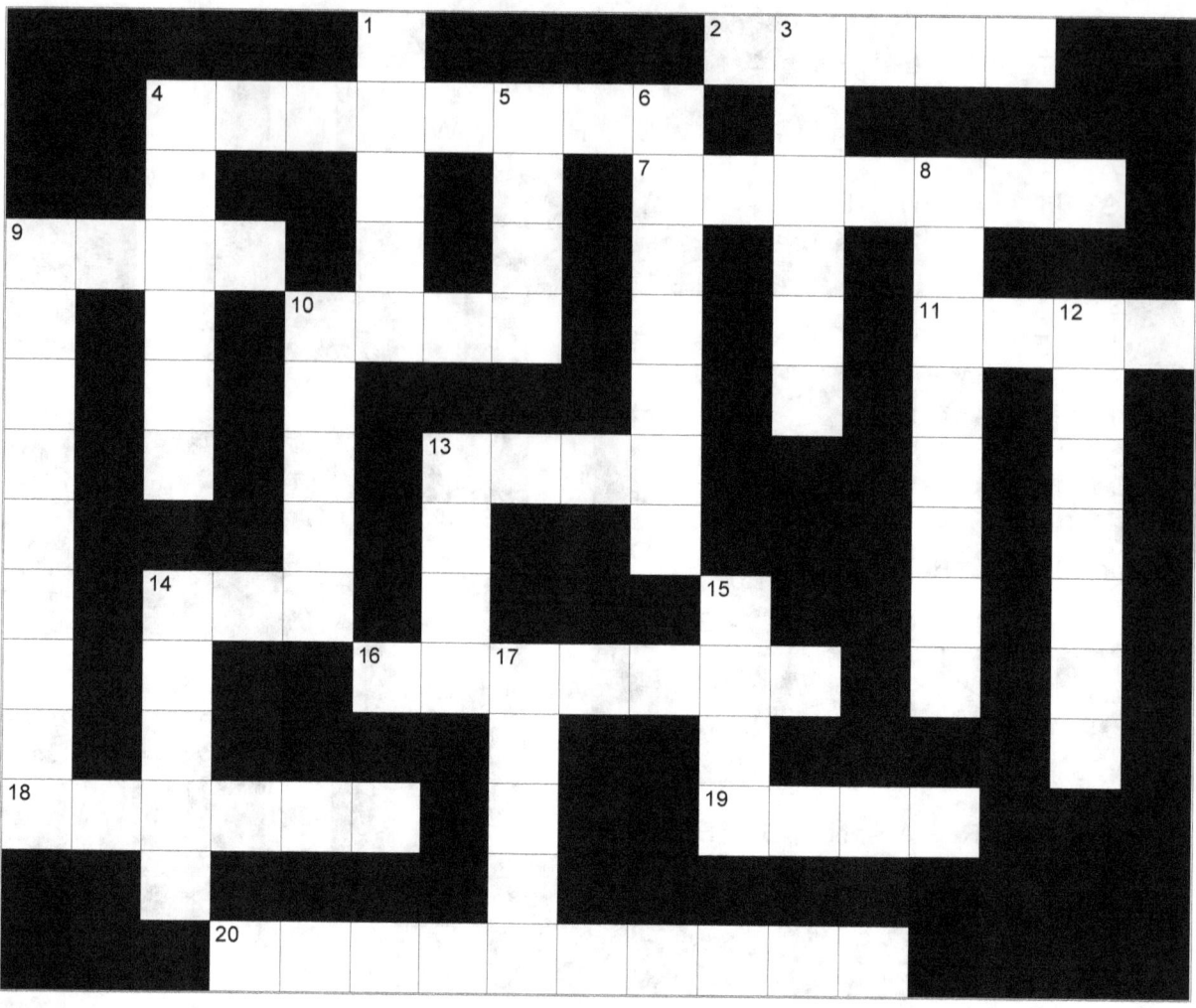

Across

2. Stanley threw it out the window.
4. Blanche seeks this in the sky.
7. Ironic apartment name; ___ Fields
9. Wedding night pajamas were made of this
10. The name DuBois means this.
11. According to Eunice, it keeps on going.
13. In Stanley's joke, the rooster stopped pursuing the hen because of this.
14. Blanche says only he could describe the Kowalskis' living conditions.
16. Blanche says she'll burn these that Stanley has touched.
18. Blanche's sister; Stanley's wife
19. He knows the gossip about Blanche.
20. According to Stella, this is Blanche's weakness.

Down

1. Blanche's astrological sign
3. Blanche's destination
4. Stanley's ethnic heritage
5. Proves home ownership
6. New Orleans
8. A woman's charm is fifty percent this.
9. Blanche depended on the kindness of ___.
10. Meaning of Blanche's name
12. The Mexican woman sells these.
13. Stanley says spousal ownership of property is the Napoleonic ___.
14. Game Stanley and the men played
15. Blanche renames the Flamingo The Tarantula ___ Hotel.
17. At the start of Scene 10 Blanche wears a white evening gown, slippers, and this.

A Streetcar Named Desire Crossword 3 Answer Key

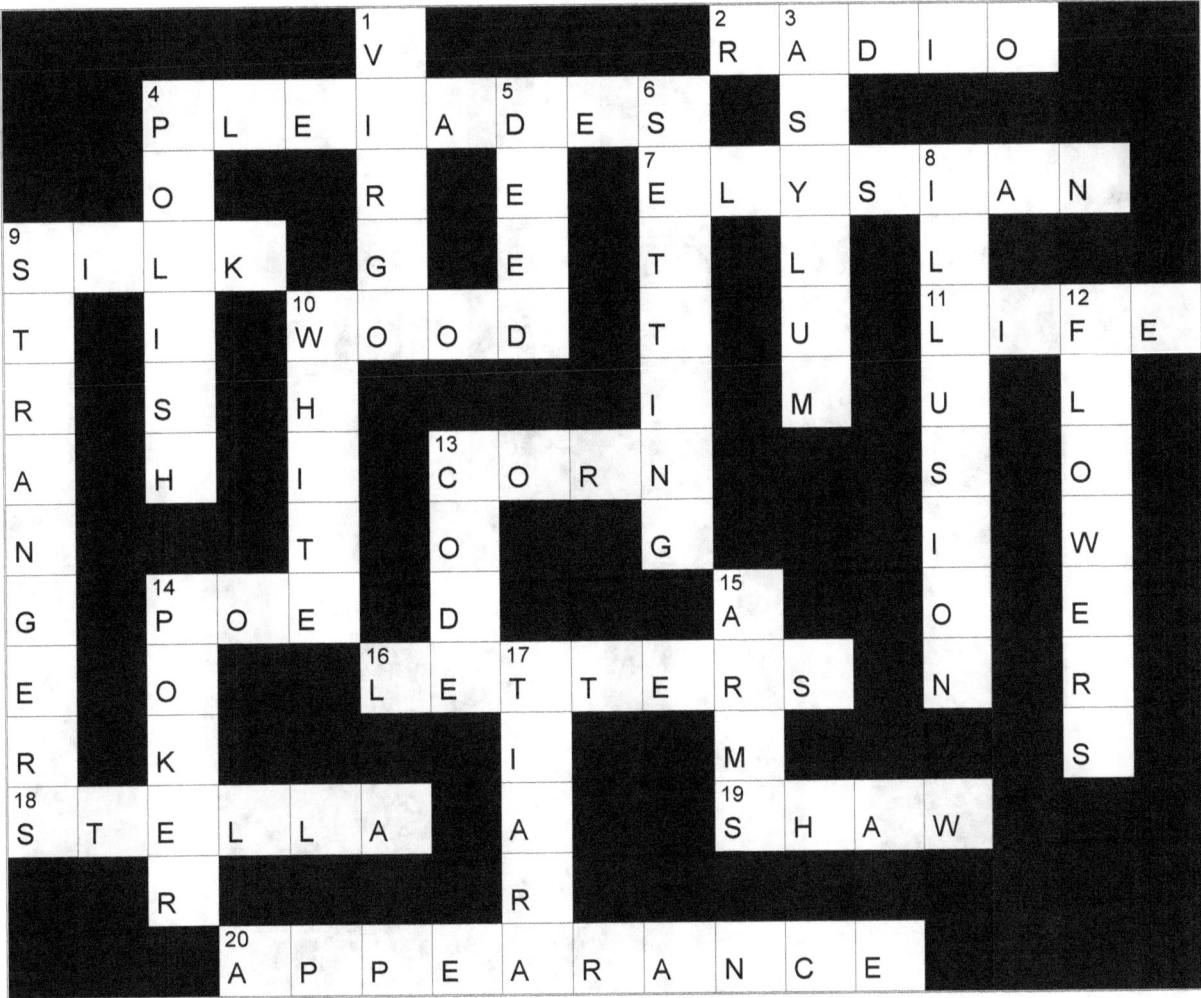

Across
2. Stanley threw it out the window.
4. Blanche seeks this in the sky.
7. Ironic apartment name; ___ Fields
9. Wedding night pajamas were made of this
10. The name DuBois means this.
11. According to Eunice, it keeps on going.
13. In Stanley's joke, the rooster stopped pursuing the hen because of this.
14. Blanche says only he could describe the Kowalskis' living conditions.
16. Blanche says she'll burn these that Stanley has touched.
18. Blanche's sister; Stanley's wife
19. He knows the gossip about Blanche.
20. According to Stella, this is Blanche's weakness.

Down
1. Blanche's astrological sign
3. Blanche's destination
4. Stanley's ethnic heritage
5. Proves home ownership
6. New Orleans
8. A woman's charm is fifty percent this.
9. Blanche depended on the kindness of ___.
10. Meaning of Blanche's name
12. The Mexican woman sells these.
13. Stanley says spousal ownership of property is the Napoleonic ___.
14. Game Stanley and the men played
15. Blanche renames the Flamingo The Tarantula ___ Hotel.
17. At the start of Scene 10 Blanche wears a white evening gown, slippers, and this.

A Streetcar Named Desire Crossword 4

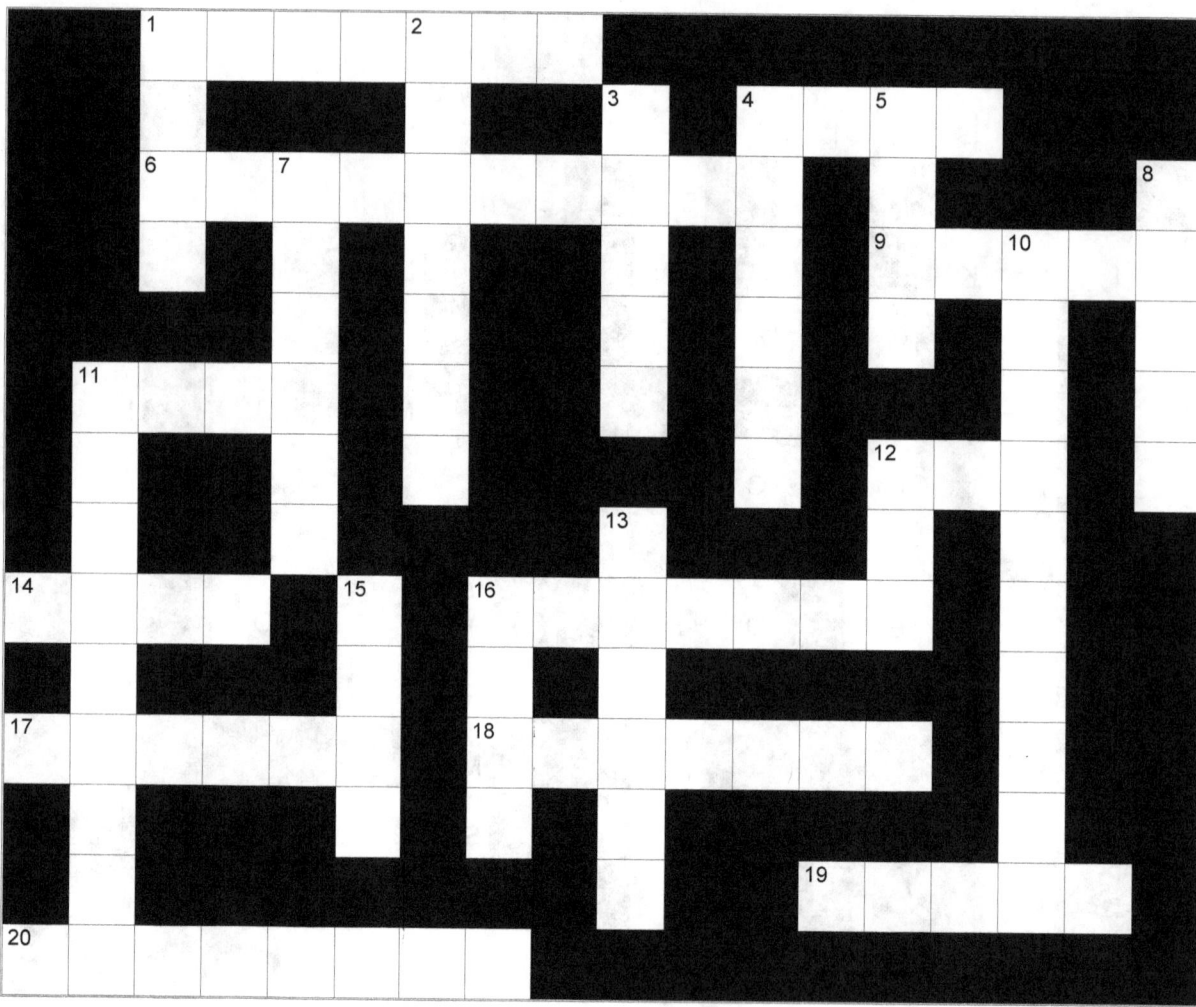

Across
1. He rapes Blanche.
4. Blanche renames the Flamingo The Tarantula ___ Hotel.
6. Stanley smashed these on the wedding night.
9. At the start of Scene 10 Blanche wears a white evening gown, slippers, and this.
11. Blanche said he sent a telegram.
12. Blanche says only he could describe the Kowalskis' living conditions.
14. Proves home ownership
16. It would make Blanche weep with joy.
17. Blanche's sister; Stanley's wife
18. The Mexican woman sells these.
19. Game Stanley and the men played
20. Stella's condition

Down
1. Wedding night pajamas were made of this
2. Blanche says she'll burn these that Stanley has touched.
3. He took his own life.
4. Blanche's destination
5. Williams compares Blanche's manner and clothing to this.
7. Blanche says eating unwashed ___ will cause her to die.
8. Stanley threw it out the window.
10. According to Stella, this is Blanche's weakness.
11. It is named Desire.
12. Stella calls Stanley a ___.
13. Mitch's real name
15. He knows the gossip about Blanche.
16. According to Eunice, it keeps on going.

A Streetcar Named Desire Crossword 4 Answer Key

Across
1. He rapes Blanche.
4. Blanche renames the Flamingo The Tarantula ___ Hotel.
6. Stanley smashed these on the wedding night.
9. At the start of Scene 10 Blanche wears a white evening gown, slippers, and this.
11. Blanche said he sent a telegram.
12. Blanche says only he could describe the Kowalskis' living conditions.
14. Proves home ownership
16. It would make Blanche weep with joy.
17. Blanche's sister; Stanley's wife
18. The Mexican woman sells these.
19. Game Stanley and the men played
20. Stella's condition

Down
1. Wedding night pajamas were made of this
2. Blanche says she'll burn these that Stanley has touched.
3. He took his own life.
4. Blanche's destination
5. Williams compares Blanche's manner and clothing to this.
7. Blanche says eating unwashed ___ will cause her to die.
8. Stanley threw it out the window.
10. According to Stella, this is Blanche's weakness.
11. It is named Desire.
12. Stella calls Stanley a ___.
13. Mitch's real name
15. He knows the gossip about Blanche.
16. According to Eunice, it keeps on going.

A Streetcar Named Desire

BUTTONS	BLANCHE	RHINESTONES	ALLAN	PIG
QUEENS	WHITE	FIRE	SETTING	ILLUSION
LIFE	RADIO	FREE SPACE	STREETCAR	WILLIAMS
ELYSIAN	DEED	STRANGERS	GRAPES	LANTERN
POE	SHEP	FLAMINGO	ARMS	TICKET

A Streetcar Named Desire

MUSIC	SILK	LEAVING	PLEIADES	MITCH
STELLA	LIGHTBULBS	CIGARETTE	CORN	APPEARANCE
SHAW	VIRGO	FREE SPACE	STANLEY	POKER
HOSPITAL	POLISH	MOTH	TIARA	CODE
EUNICE	BOTTLE	WOOD	FLOWERS	LETTERS

A Streetcar Named Desire

PREGNANT	PIG	STANLEY	SHAW	FLAMINGO
RHINESTONES	EUNICE	RADIO	ARMS	PLEIADES
APPEARANCE	FIRE	FREE SPACE	HOSPITAL	LETTERS
POKER	SETTING	LANTERN	CODE	ASYLUM
ALLAN	BOTTLE	BLANCHE	STRANGERS	LIGHTBULBS

A Streetcar Named Desire

ELYSIAN	SHEP	MOTH	LIFE	VIRGO
POE	STELLA	WOOD	MITCH	QUEENS
BELLE	POLISH	FREE SPACE	TIARA	SILK
MUSIC	STREETCAR	BUTTONS	CIGARETTE	HAROLD
ILLUSION	WILLIAMS	GRAPES	TICKET	LEAVING

A Streetcar Named Desire

ARMS	FLAMINGO	STREETCAR	WILLIAMS	POKER
RADIO	RHINESTONES	BOTTLE	LEAVING	ELYSIAN
BUTTONS	VIRGO	FREE SPACE	TIARA	LANTERN
BELLE	LIFE	SHEP	DEED	POLISH
HOSPITAL	QUEENS	CORN	CIGARETTE	STELLA

A Streetcar Named Desire

PLEIADES	MUSIC	TICKET	APPEARANCE	ILLUSION
SILK	EUNICE	STRANGERS	LETTERS	GRAPES
ASYLUM	FLOWERS	FREE SPACE	SETTING	POE
WHITE	PREGNANT	MOTH	HAROLD	STANLEY
SHAW	BLANCHE	ALLAN	CODE	LIGHTBULBS

A Streetcar Named Desire

SILK	STREETCAR	APPEARANCE	CODE	LANTERN
CORN	BELLE	VIRGO	RADIO	STRANGERS
FLAMINGO	MOTH	FREE SPACE	POE	ILLUSION
HAROLD	BLANCHE	LETTERS	HOSPITAL	QUEENS
STELLA	ALLAN	FLOWERS	STANLEY	SHAW

A Streetcar Named Desire

EUNICE	TIARA	POLISH	FIRE	ARMS
PLEIADES	WHITE	ASYLUM	WOOD	WILLIAMS
PREGNANT	DEED	FREE SPACE	BUTTONS	POKER
GRAPES	BOTTLE	CIGARETTE	ELYSIAN	RHINESTONES
PIG	SHEP	MITCH	SETTING	LIGHTBULBS

A Streetcar Named Desire

SETTING	TIARA	LANTERN	ARMS	HAROLD
ILLUSION	BOTTLE	LEAVING	GRAPES	RADIO
STANLEY	EUNICE	FREE SPACE	PLEIADES	FIRE
POLISH	POKER	LETTERS	POE	STRANGERS
FLOWERS	ALLAN	STELLA	FLAMINGO	MOTH

A Streetcar Named Desire

WHITE	HOSPITAL	PREGNANT	STREETCAR	SILK
VIRGO	TICKET	ELYSIAN	LIFE	SHEP
QUEENS	LIGHTBULBS	FREE SPACE	BLANCHE	CODE
WILLIAMS	MUSIC	BUTTONS	APPEARANCE	BELLE
PIG	DEED	ASYLUM	CIGARETTE	MITCH

A Streetcar Named Desire

WOOD	LIGHTBULBS	PIG	EUNICE	QUEENS
SHAW	SHEP	HOSPITAL	LANTERN	TICKET
FLOWERS	SETTING	FREE SPACE	LETTERS	DEED
LEAVING	BLANCHE	MUSIC	ARMS	BOTTLE
WILLIAMS	GRAPES	VIRGO	RHINESTONES	POE

A Streetcar Named Desire

HAROLD	PREGNANT	ILLUSION	STANLEY	TIARA
WHITE	PLEIADES	CIGARETTE	STREETCAR	APPEARANCE
POLISH	SILK	FREE SPACE	BUTTONS	MOTH
POKER	ASYLUM	BELLE	ALLAN	STELLA
RADIO	CORN	STRANGERS	MITCH	FLAMINGO

A Streetcar Named Desire

PLEIADES	BUTTONS	TIARA	CORN	STRANGERS
MOTH	ASYLUM	TICKET	WILLIAMS	QUEENS
RHINESTONES	HOSPITAL	FREE SPACE	WOOD	SHEP
ELYSIAN	LIFE	BELLE	MITCH	POLISH
APPEARANCE	WHITE	ARMS	VIRGO	LANTERN

A Streetcar Named Desire

BLANCHE	POE	STELLA	BOTTLE	DEED
ILLUSION	MUSIC	ALLAN	FLAMINGO	CIGARETTE
LIGHTBULBS	PIG	FREE SPACE	LEAVING	SILK
HAROLD	FIRE	SHAW	CODE	STREETCAR
FLOWERS	GRAPES	STANLEY	EUNICE	POKER

A Streetcar Named Desire

CORN	RHINESTONES	MUSIC	LANTERN	FLOWERS
WHITE	STANLEY	BLANCHE	HOSPITAL	SHEP
SILK	PIG	FREE SPACE	ASYLUM	WOOD
TICKET	BUTTONS	POLISH	PREGNANT	LEAVING
POKER	CIGARETTE	FLAMINGO	POE	SETTING

A Streetcar Named Desire

WILLIAMS	ELYSIAN	BELLE	LIGHTBULBS	MITCH
FIRE	RADIO	EUNICE	PLEIADES	TIARA
STRANGERS	QUEENS	FREE SPACE	LETTERS	STELLA
ILLUSION	GRAPES	VIRGO	CODE	BOTTLE
DEED	MOTH	APPEARANCE	SHAW	STREETCAR

A Streetcar Named Desire

LIGHTBULBS	GRAPES	ILLUSION	WOOD	CORN
SILK	EUNICE	SHAW	RHINESTONES	ARMS
FLAMINGO	MOTH	FREE SPACE	LIFE	TIARA
FLOWERS	STELLA	ASYLUM	QUEENS	PLEIADES
SETTING	PIG	HAROLD	CODE	CIGARETTE

A Streetcar Named Desire

PREGNANT	RADIO	APPEARANCE	POLISH	LANTERN
BUTTONS	MITCH	WHITE	FIRE	WILLIAMS
MUSIC	VIRGO	FREE SPACE	ALLAN	ELYSIAN
POKER	STRANGERS	DEED	BOTTLE	STANLEY
BELLE	LEAVING	SHEP	HOSPITAL	BLANCHE

A Streetcar Named Desire

POKER	CODE	MOTH	POLISH	WOOD
DEED	ALLAN	SETTING	WILLIAMS	HAROLD
STANLEY	POE	FREE SPACE	PREGNANT	RADIO
PIG	LETTERS	SILK	ARMS	ELYSIAN
LANTERN	GRAPES	BOTTLE	STRANGERS	EUNICE

A Streetcar Named Desire

CORN	MUSIC	PLEIADES	QUEENS	LEAVING
CIGARETTE	ASYLUM	LIGHTBULBS	SHEP	BELLE
TICKET	VIRGO	FREE SPACE	BUTTONS	APPEARANCE
BLANCHE	HOSPITAL	FIRE	LIFE	FLOWERS
TIARA	SHAW	FLAMINGO	STREETCAR	RHINESTONES

A Streetcar Named Desire

GRAPES	LEAVING	EUNICE	DEED	ALLAN
STANLEY	FLAMINGO	MITCH	WOOD	ARMS
STREETCAR	RADIO	FREE SPACE	FIRE	VIRGO
POE	STRANGERS	LIGHTBULBS	MUSIC	LETTERS
BLANCHE	STELLA	HAROLD	WILLIAMS	FLOWERS

A Streetcar Named Desire

SETTING	ELYSIAN	LANTERN	BELLE	TIARA
APPEARANCE	SHEP	ASYLUM	HOSPITAL	SILK
ILLUSION	QUEENS	FREE SPACE	LIFE	CIGARETTE
MOTH	CODE	PREGNANT	BUTTONS	RHINESTONES
WHITE	POKER	CORN	POLISH	TICKET

A Streetcar Named Desire

LANTERN	RHINESTONES	FLAMINGO	POLISH	LETTERS
LIGHTBULBS	CIGARETTE	LEAVING	TICKET	POKER
CODE	QUEENS	FREE SPACE	STANLEY	STREETCAR
FIRE	SHEP	ALLAN	PLEIADES	MITCH
ASYLUM	MOTH	ILLUSION	PIG	APPEARANCE

A Streetcar Named Desire

BLANCHE	HOSPITAL	RADIO	MUSIC	ARMS
DEED	BELLE	BOTTLE	WILLIAMS	BUTTONS
SHAW	PREGNANT	FREE SPACE	WOOD	VIRGO
CORN	STRANGERS	ELYSIAN	TIARA	WHITE
HAROLD	GRAPES	FLOWERS	STELLA	EUNICE

A Streetcar Named Desire

STREETCAR	BUTTONS	CODE	QUEENS	BLANCHE
RHINESTONES	POE	TIARA	RADIO	MITCH
ILLUSION	LEAVING	FREE SPACE	PIG	DEED
LIGHTBULBS	EUNICE	WILLIAMS	LANTERN	FLOWERS
ALLAN	STELLA	SHAW	SHEP	SILK

A Streetcar Named Desire

POLISH	TICKET	WOOD	ELYSIAN	FIRE
SETTING	BOTTLE	MOTH	LIFE	BELLE
PREGNANT	APPEARANCE	FREE SPACE	WHITE	HOSPITAL
STRANGERS	LETTERS	FLAMINGO	ARMS	PLEIADES
CORN	POKER	STANLEY	GRAPES	MUSIC

Copyrighted

A Streetcar Named Desire

PREGNANT	GRAPES	PLEIADES	RADIO	MUSIC
FLAMINGO	BOTTLE	STREETCAR	FLOWERS	TICKET
ELYSIAN	WHITE	FREE SPACE	LIGHTBULBS	APPEARANCE
LIFE	DEED	CORN	LANTERN	STANLEY
STELLA	HAROLD	BUTTONS	LETTERS	CODE

A Streetcar Named Desire

WOOD	SILK	STRANGERS	FIRE	MOTH
SETTING	ILLUSION	ARMS	ASYLUM	EUNICE
MITCH	TIARA	FREE SPACE	SHAW	POE
PIG	LEAVING	RHINESTONES	QUEENS	POKER
POLISH	BLANCHE	HOSPITAL	SHEP	CIGARETTE

A Streetcar Named Desire

LETTERS	BLANCHE	GRAPES	STRANGERS	PLEIADES
BELLE	APPEARANCE	MOTH	PREGNANT	SHEP
FIRE	WHITE	FREE SPACE	ALLAN	HAROLD
CIGARETTE	WOOD	FLAMINGO	PIG	DEED
BUTTONS	RADIO	TICKET	STREETCAR	CORN

A Streetcar Named Desire

STELLA	MITCH	VIRGO	LEAVING	LIGHTBULBS
QUEENS	BOTTLE	SHAW	RHINESTONES	TIARA
EUNICE	CODE	FREE SPACE	POLISH	WILLIAMS
SETTING	LANTERN	POKER	FLOWERS	MUSIC
SILK	LIFE	ARMS	STANLEY	POE

A Streetcar Named Desire

BLANCHE	POE	CIGARETTE	MUSIC	SHAW
DEED	MITCH	ARMS	BOTTLE	CORN
ELYSIAN	POLISH	FREE SPACE	WOOD	PLEIADES
EUNICE	ILLUSION	RHINESTONES	STREETCAR	LIGHTBULBS
LIFE	RADIO	SHEP	LEAVING	SETTING

A Streetcar Named Desire

WHITE	STRANGERS	LETTERS	HOSPITAL	LANTERN
GRAPES	ASYLUM	ALLAN	SILK	BELLE
CODE	FLAMINGO	FREE SPACE	MOTH	PREGNANT
QUEENS	TIARA	FIRE	APPEARANCE	STELLA
WILLIAMS	VIRGO	BUTTONS	TICKET	HAROLD

A Streetcar Named Desire Vocabulary

No.	Word	Clue/Definition
1.	AMIABILITY	Friendliness
2.	ANTIQUITY	Ancient times
3.	BASHFUL	Shy
4.	BEAMS	Radiates
5.	BELLOWING	Roaring
6.	BESTIAL	Inhuman
7.	CALLOUS	Insensitive
8.	CLEFT	Hollowed area
9.	COARSE	Natural; unprocessed
10.	COMMON	Ordinary
11.	COSMOPOLITAN	Worldly
12.	CULTIVATED	Tended
13.	DEED	Document of ownership
14.	DEMURENESS	Modesty
15.	DEPLETION	Scarcity
16.	DESTITUTE	Without necessities; poor
17.	DIFFIDENT	Timid
18.	DIVESTED	Got rid of
19.	DOPE	Gossip
20.	EFFEMINATE	Feminine
21.	ELATED	Happy
22.	EXHILARATION	Feeling of stimulation
23.	EXPRESSIONS	Sayings
24.	EXTRACTION	Lineage; from what people one has come
25.	FEIGNED	Pretended
26.	GANDER	Look
27.	GAUDY	Showy
28.	GOSSAMER	Delicate fabric
29.	GRAVELY	Seriously
30.	GROTESQUE	Unnatural or ugly
31.	HECTIC	Chaotic
32.	HETEROGENEOUS	Different
33.	HOARSELY	With a strained voice
34.	HUNCHED	Bent over; crouched
35.	IMMEASURABLY	Vast
36.	IMPROVIDENT	Lacking judgment
37.	INCONGRUOUS	Out of place
38.	INDECENT	Improper
39.	INDIFFERENCE	Lack of concern
40.	INDISTINGUISHABLE	Not understandable; not clear
41.	INDOLENT	Lazy
42.	INEFFECTUAL	Unsatisfactory; not effective
43.	INERT	Unable to move or act
44.	INSUFFERABLY	Unbearably
45.	LAPPING	Drinking up, like a dog
46.	LURID	Horrible
47.	MALARKEY	Foolish talk
48.	MENACING	Threatening
49.	NOCTURNAL	During darkness
50.	NOTION	Idea
51.	OMINOUSLY	Threateningly

A Streetcar Named Desire Vocabulary

No.	Word	Clue/Definition
52.	PERPETRATED	Committed
53.	PERPETUAL	Never ending
54.	PERPLEXITY	Confusion or uncertainty
55.	PINION	Wrestle; hold down
56.	PITCH	Set talk designed to persuade
57.	PORTIERES	Heavy curtains
58.	PRIM	Stiffly proper or precise in manner or appearance
59.	PRIMITIVE	Like early mankind
60.	PRODIGIOUSLY	Wonderfully
61.	RAFFISH	Vulgar
62.	RECKON	Figure
63.	REDOLENCE	Odor; fragrance
64.	REFLECTIVELY	Thoughtfully
65.	REPERTOIRE	Collection
66.	REPROACH	Blame
67.	RETREATING	Going backwards
68.	REVERBERATED	Echoed
69.	RHUMBA	Cuban dance
70.	ROW	Fight
71.	SACCHARINE	Overly sweet
72.	SENTIMENTAL	Emotional
73.	SERENELY	Calmly
74.	SINISTER	Evil
75.	SINUOUSLY	Curving or twisting
76.	SOLEMN	Serious
77.	SPECTRAL	Ghostly
78.	SUFFICIENT	Enough
79.	SWINDLE	Scam
80.	TEMPERAMENTAL	Unpredictable; not consistent
81.	TRANQUILITY	Peace
82.	TRANSITORY	Temporary
83.	UNCAVALIER	Discourteous
84.	UNCOUTH	Crude; rough; unpolished
85.	VALISE	Suitcase
86.	VIVACITY	Liveliness
87.	VIVID	Intense
88.	VOLUPTUOUSLY	Sensuously
89.	YEARNINGLY	With desire

A Streetcar Named Desire Vocabulary Fill In The Blanks 1

_____ 1. Lack of concern

_____ 2. Chaotic

_____ 3. Improper

_____ 4. Pretended

_____ 5. Happy

_____ 6. Confusion or uncertainty

_____ 7. Seriously

_____ 8. Blame

_____ 9. Vulgar

_____ 10. Ordinary

_____ 11. Not understandable; not clear

_____ 12. Radiates

_____ 13. Ghostly

_____ 14. Inhuman

_____ 15. Curving or twisting

_____ 16. Lazy

_____ 17. Timid

_____ 18. Calmly

_____ 19. Feeling of stimulation

_____ 20. Sensuously

A Streetcar Named Desire Vocabulary Fill In The Blanks 1 Answer Key

INDIFFERENCE	1. Lack of concern
HECTIC	2. Chaotic
INDECENT	3. Improper
FEIGNED	4. Pretended
ELATED	5. Happy
PERPLEXITY	6. Confusion or uncertainty
GRAVELY	7. Seriously
REPROACH	8. Blame
RAFFISH	9. Vulgar
COMMON	10. Ordinary
INDISTINGUISHABLE	11. Not understandable; not clear
BEAMS	12. Radiates
SPECTRAL	13. Ghostly
BESTIAL	14. Inhuman
SINUOUSLY	15. Curving or twisting
INDOLENT	16. Lazy
DIFFIDENT	17. Timid
SERENELY	18. Calmly
EXHILARATION	19. Feeling of stimulation
VOLUPTUOUSLY	20. Sensuously

A Streetcar Named Desire Vocabulary Fill In The Blanks 2

_____	1. Roaring
_____	2. Scam
_____	3. Wonderfully
_____	4. Thoughtfully
_____	5. Showy
_____	6. Fight
_____	7. Calmly
_____	8. Inhuman
_____	9. Threatening
_____	10. Overly sweet
_____	11. With desire
_____	12. Threateningly
_____	13. Lack of concern
_____	14. Committed
_____	15. Hollowed area
_____	16. Got rid of
_____	17. Echoed
_____	18. Happy
_____	19. Vulgar
_____	20. Different

A Streetcar Named Desire Vocabulary Fill In The Blanks 2 Answer Key

BELLOWING	1. Roaring
SWINDLE	2. Scam
PRODIGIOUSLY	3. Wonderfully
REFLECTIVELY	4. Thoughtfully
GAUDY	5. Showy
ROW	6. Fight
SERENELY	7. Calmly
BESTIAL	8. Inhuman
MENACING	9. Threatening
SACCHARINE	10. Overly sweet
YEARNINGLY	11. With desire
OMINOUSLY	12. Threateningly
INDIFFERENCE	13. Lack of concern
PERPETRATED	14. Committed
CLEFT	15. Hollowed area
DIVESTED	16. Got rid of
REVERBERATED	17. Echoed
ELATED	18. Happy
RAFFISH	19. Vulgar
HETEROGENEOUS	20. Different

A Streetcar Named Desire Vocabulary Fill In The Blanks 3

_____

1. Unnatural or ugly
2. Delicate fabric
3. Overly sweet
4. Calmly
5. Suitcase
6. Odor; fragrance
7. Serious
8. Ancient times
9. Not understandable; not clear
10. Timid
11. Collection
12. With a strained voice
13. Modesty
14. Roaring
15. Feminine
16. Echoed
17. Foolish talk
18. Peace
19. Vulgar
20. Emotional

A Streetcar Named Desire Vocabulary Fill In The Blanks 3 Answer Key

GROTESQUE	1. Unnatural or ugly
GOSSAMER	2. Delicate fabric
SACCHARINE	3. Overly sweet
SERENELY	4. Calmly
VALISE	5. Suitcase
REDOLENCE	6. Odor; fragrance
SOLEMN	7. Serious
ANTIQUITY	8. Ancient times
INDISTINGUISHABLE	9. Not understandable; not clear
DIFFIDENT	10. Timid
REPERTOIRE	11. Collection
HOARSELY	12. With a strained voice
DEMURENESS	13. Modesty
BELLOWING	14. Roaring
EFFEMINATE	15. Feminine
REVERBERATED	16. Echoed
MALARKEY	17. Foolish talk
TRANQUILITY	18. Peace
RAFFISH	19. Vulgar
SENTIMENTAL	20. Emotional

A Streetcar Named Desire Vocabulary Fill In The Blanks 4

_____   1. Inhuman

_____   2. Bent over; crouched

_____   3. Wrestle; hold down

_____   4. Sensuously

_____   5. Unnatural or ugly

_____   6. Scam

_____   7. Peace

_____   8. Insensitive

_____   9. Foolish talk

_____   10. Tended

_____   11. Timid

_____   12. Committed

_____   13. With a strained voice

_____   14. Enough

_____   15. Unpredictable; not consistent

_____   16. Gossip

_____   17. Odor; fragrance

_____   18. Improper

_____   19. Temporary

_____   20. Confusion or uncertainty

A Streetcar Named Desire Vocabulary Fill In The Blanks 4 Answer Key

BESTIAL	1. Inhuman
HUNCHED	2. Bent over; crouched
PINION	3. Wrestle; hold down
VOLUPTUOUSLY	4. Sensuously
GROTESQUE	5. Unnatural or ugly
SWINDLE	6. Scam
TRANQUILITY	7. Peace
CALLOUS	8. Insensitive
MALARKEY	9. Foolish talk
CULTIVATED	10. Tended
DIFFIDENT	11. Timid
PERPETRATED	12. Committed
HOARSELY	13. With a strained voice
SUFFICIENT	14. Enough
TEMPERAMENTAL	15. Unpredictable; not consistent
DOPE	16. Gossip
REDOLENCE	17. Odor; fragrance
INDECENT	18. Improper
TRANSITORY	19. Temporary
PERPLEXITY	20. Confusion or uncertainty

A Streetcar Named Desire Vocabulary Matching 1

___ 1. INDECENT
___ 2. TRANSITORY
___ 3. DESTITUTE
___ 4. OMINOUSLY
___ 5. DEPLETION
___ 6. PITCH
___ 7. RAFFISH
___ 8. RHUMBA
___ 9. PERPETRATED
___ 10. EXPRESSIONS
___ 11. INDIFFERENCE
___ 12. PRIMITIVE
___ 13. ANTIQUITY
___ 14. GOSSAMER
___ 15. SWINDLE
___ 16. REFLECTIVELY
___ 17. BEAMS
___ 18. HOARSELY
___ 19. NOTION
___ 20. IMMEASURABLY
___ 21. NOCTURNAL
___ 22. SUFFICIENT
___ 23. PRIM
___ 24. LURID
___ 25. UNCOUTH

A. Enough
B. Scarcity
C. During darkness
D. Ancient times
E. Idea
F. Lack of concern
G. Set talk designed to persuade
H. Radiates
I. Sayings
J. Stiffly proper or precise in manner or appearance
K. Vast
L. Without necessities; poor
M. Temporary
N. Horrible
O. Cuban dance
P. Improper
Q. Delicate fabric
R. Like early mankind
S. Vulgar
T. With a strained voice
U. Scam
V. Thoughtfully
W. Committed
X. Crude; rough; unpolished
Y. Threateningly

A Streetcar Named Desire Vocabulary Matching 1 Answer Key

P - 1. INDECENT	A.	Enough
M - 2. TRANSITORY	B.	Scarcity
L - 3. DESTITUTE	C.	During darkness
Y - 4. OMINOUSLY	D.	Ancient times
B - 5. DEPLETION	E.	Idea
G - 6. PITCH	F.	Lack of concern
S - 7. RAFFISH	G.	Set talk designed to persuade
O - 8. RHUMBA	H.	Radiates
W - 9. PERPETRATED	I.	Sayings
I - 10. EXPRESSIONS	J.	Stiffly proper or precise in manner or appearance
F - 11. INDIFFERENCE	K.	Vast
R - 12. PRIMITIVE	L.	Without necessities; poor
D - 13. ANTIQUITY	M.	Temporary
Q - 14. GOSSAMER	N.	Horrible
U - 15. SWINDLE	O.	Cuban dance
V - 16. REFLECTIVELY	P.	Improper
H - 17. BEAMS	Q.	Delicate fabric
T - 18. HOARSELY	R.	Like early mankind
E - 19. NOTION	S.	Vulgar
K - 20. IMMEASURABLY	T.	With a strained voice
C - 21. NOCTURNAL	U.	Scam
A - 22. SUFFICIENT	V.	Thoughtfully
J - 23. PRIM	W.	Committed
N - 24. LURID	X.	Crude; rough; unpolished
X - 25. UNCOUTH	Y.	Threateningly

A Streetcar Named Desire Vocabulary Matching 2

___ 1. UNCAVALIER   A. Lacking judgment
___ 2. CULTIVATED   B. Feeling of stimulation
___ 3. YEARNINGLY   C. Echoed
___ 4. SOLEMN   D. Not understandable; not clear
___ 5. EXHILARATION   E. Sayings
___ 6. HUNCHED   F. Discourteous
___ 7. VIVACITY   G. With desire
___ 8. COMMON   H. Bent over; crouched
___ 9. VOLUPTUOUSLY   I. Document of ownership
___10. ANTIQUITY   J. Ordinary
___11. TRANQUILITY   K. Ancient times
___12. BASHFUL   L. Shy
___13. EXPRESSIONS   M. Calmly
___14. VALISE   N. Collection
___15. EXTRACTION   O. Sensuously
___16. CLEFT   P. Serious
___17. SERENELY   Q. Lineage; from what people one has come
___18. INEFFECTUAL   R. Suitcase
___19. IMPROVIDENT   S. Liveliness
___20. REPERTOIRE   T. Tended
___21. INDIFFERENCE   U. Unsatisfactory; not effective
___22. DEED   V. Hollowed area
___23. REVERBERATED   W. Threateningly
___24. INDISTINGUISHABLE   X. Peace
___25. OMINOUSLY   Y. Lack of concern

A Streetcar Named Desire Vocabulary Matching 2 Answer Key

F - 1. UNCAVALIER
T - 2. CULTIVATED
G - 3. YEARNINGLY
P - 4. SOLEMN
B - 5. EXHILARATION
H - 6. HUNCHED
S - 7. VIVACITY
J - 8. COMMON
O - 9. VOLUPTUOUSLY
K - 10. ANTIQUITY
X - 11. TRANQUILITY
L - 12. BASHFUL
E - 13. EXPRESSIONS
R - 14. VALISE
Q - 15. EXTRACTION
V - 16. CLEFT
M - 17. SERENELY
U - 18. INEFFECTUAL
A - 19. IMPROVIDENT
N - 20. REPERTOIRE
Y - 21. INDIFFERENCE
I - 22. DEED
C - 23. REVERBERATED
D - 24. INDISTINGUISHABLE
W - 25. OMINOUSLY

A. Lacking judgment
B. Feeling of stimulation
C. Echoed
D. Not understandable; not clear
E. Sayings
F. Discourteous
G. With desire
H. Bent over; crouched
I. Document of ownership
J. Ordinary
K. Ancient times
L. Shy
M. Calmly
N. Collection
O. Sensuously
P. Serious
Q. Lineage; from what people one has come
R. Suitcase
S. Liveliness
T. Tended
U. Unsatisfactory; not effective
V. Hollowed area
W. Threateningly
X. Peace
Y. Lack of concern

A Streetcar Named Desire Vocabulary Matching 3

___ 1. INSUFFERABLY   A. Look
___ 2. ANTIQUITY   B. Foolish talk
___ 3. INEFFECTUAL   C. Showy
___ 4. REPERTOIRE   D. Peace
___ 5. SPECTRAL   E. Odor; fragrance
___ 6. PRIM   F. Insensitive
___ 7. PRIMITIVE   G. Stiffly proper or precise in manner or appearance
___ 8. PITCH   H. Unsatisfactory; not effective
___ 9. PINION   I. Ancient times
___10. SINISTER   J. Collection
___11. GAUDY   K. Wonderfully
___12. DEPLETION   L. Lacking judgment
___13. AMIABILITY   M. Evil
___14. LAPPING   N. Drinking up, like a dog
___15. GANDER   O. Wrestle; hold down
___16. TRANQUILITY   P. Ghostly
___17. IMPROVIDENT   Q. Like early mankind
___18. PRODIGIOUSLY   R. Friendliness
___19. BASHFUL   S. Shy
___20. MALARKEY   T. Unbearably
___21. CALLOUS   U. Threatening
___22. REDOLENCE   V. Worldly
___23. COSMOPOLITAN   W. Intense
___24. VIVID   X. Set talk designed to persuade
___25. MENACING   Y. Scarcity

A Streetcar Named Desire Vocabulary Matching 3 Answer Key

T - 1. INSUFFERABLY
I - 2. ANTIQUITY
H - 3. INEFFECTUAL
J - 4. REPERTOIRE
P - 5. SPECTRAL
G - 6. PRIM
Q - 7. PRIMITIVE
X - 8. PITCH
O - 9. PINION
M -10. SINISTER
C -11. GAUDY
Y -12. DEPLETION
R -13. AMIABILITY
N -14. LAPPING
A -15. GANDER
D -16. TRANQUILITY
L -17. IMPROVIDENT
K -18. PRODIGIOUSLY
S -19. BASHFUL
B -20. MALARKEY
F -21. CALLOUS
E -22. REDOLENCE
V -23. COSMOPOLITAN
W -24. VIVID
U -25. MENACING

A. Look
B. Foolish talk
C. Showy
D. Peace
E. Odor; fragrance
F. Insensitive
G. Stiffly proper or precise in manner or appearance
H. Unsatisfactory; not effective
I. Ancient times
J. Collection
K. Wonderfully
L. Lacking judgment
M. Evil
N. Drinking up, like a dog
O. Wrestle; hold down
P. Ghostly
Q. Like early mankind
R. Friendliness
S. Shy
T. Unbearably
U. Threatening
V. Worldly
W. Intense
X. Set talk designed to persuade
Y. Scarcity

A Streetcar Named Desire Vocabulary Matching 4

___ 1. NOCTURNAL   A. Set talk designed to persuade
___ 2. EXPRESSIONS   B. Committed
___ 3. SENTIMENTAL   C. Look
___ 4. PRIM   D. Unnatural or ugly
___ 5. VIVID   E. During darkness
___ 6. INEFFECTUAL   F. Lazy
___ 7. LAPPING   G. Discourteous
___ 8. UNCAVALIER   H. Natural; unprocessed
___ 9. MALARKEY   I. Foolish talk
___10. RHUMBA   J. Happy
___11. GANDER   K. Unsatisfactory; not effective
___12. BELLOWING   L. Stiffly proper or precise in manner or appearance
___13. GROTESQUE   M. Going backwards
___14. ELATED   N. Gossip
___15. SACCHARINE   O. Liveliness
___16. VIVACITY   P. Intense
___17. PITCH   Q. Emotional
___18. CULTIVATED   R. Overly sweet
___19. OMINOUSLY   S. Tended
___20. RETREATING   T. Cuban dance
___21. GOSSAMER   U. Roaring
___22. PERPETRATED   V. Delicate fabric
___23. COARSE   W. Threateningly
___24. DOPE   X. Sayings
___25. INDOLENT   Y. Drinking up, like a dog

A Streetcar Named Desire Vocabulary Matching 4 Answer Key

E - 1. NOCTURNAL	A.	Set talk designed to persuade
X - 2. EXPRESSIONS	B.	Committed
Q - 3. SENTIMENTAL	C.	Look
L - 4. PRIM	D.	Unnatural or ugly
P - 5. VIVID	E.	During darkness
K - 6. INEFFECTUAL	F.	Lazy
Y - 7. LAPPING	G.	Discourteous
G - 8. UNCAVALIER	H.	Natural; unprocessed
I - 9. MALARKEY	I.	Foolish talk
T - 10. RHUMBA	J.	Happy
C - 11. GANDER	K.	Unsatisfactory; not effective
U - 12. BELLOWING	L.	Stiffly proper or precise in manner or appearance
D - 13. GROTESQUE	M.	Going backwards
J - 14. ELATED	N.	Gossip
R - 15. SACCHARINE	O.	Liveliness
O - 16. VIVACITY	P.	Intense
A - 17. PITCH	Q.	Emotional
S - 18. CULTIVATED	R.	Overly sweet
W - 19. OMINOUSLY	S.	Tended
M - 20. RETREATING	T.	Cuban dance
V - 21. GOSSAMER	U.	Roaring
B - 22. PERPETRATED	V.	Delicate fabric
H - 23. COARSE	W.	Threateningly
N - 24. DOPE	X.	Sayings
F - 25. INDOLENT	Y.	Drinking up, like a dog

A Streetcar Named Desire Vocabulary Magic Squares 1

Match the definition with the vocabulary word. Put your answers in the magic squares below. When your answers are correct, all columns and rows will add to the same number.

A. DEPLETION
B. NOCTURNAL
C. DOPE
D. PRIMITIVE
E. TEMPERAMENTAL
F. DEMURENESS
G. INSUFFERABLY
H. UNCAVALIER
I. COMMON
J. BEAMS
K. UNCOUTH
L. DIFFIDENT
M. HOARSELY
N. REPROACH
O. LURID
P. TRANSITORY

1. Horrible
2. Radiates
3. Discourteous
4. Scarcity
5. Like early mankind
6. Unpredictable; not consistent
7. Crude; rough; unpolished
8. Blame
9. Modesty
10. Gossip
11. With a strained voice
12. Timid
13. Ordinary
14. Temporary
15. During darkness
16. Unbearably

A= 4	B= 15	C= 10	D= 5
E= 6	F= 9	G= 16	H= 3
I= 13	J= 2	K= 7	L= 12
M= 11	N= 8	O= 1	P= 14

A Streetcar Named Desire Vocabulary Magic Squares 1 Answer Key

Match the definition with the vocabulary word. Put your answers in the magic squares below. When your answers are correct, all columns and rows will add to the same number.

A. DEPLETION
B. NOCTURNAL
C. DOPE
D. PRIMITIVE
E. TEMPERAMENTAL
F. DEMURENESS
G. INSUFFERABLY
H. UNCAVALIER
I. COMMON
J. BEAMS
K. UNCOUTH
L. DIFFIDENT
M. HOARSELY
N. REPROACH
O. LURID
P. TRANSITORY

1. Horrible
2. Radiates
3. Discourteous
4. Scarcity
5. Like early mankind
6. Unpredictable; not consistent
7. Crude; rough; unpolished
8. Blame
9. Modesty
10. Gossip
11. With a strained voice
12. Timid
13. Ordinary
14. Temporary
15. During darkness
16. Unbearably

A=4	B=15	C=10	D=5
E=6	F=9	G=16	H=3
I=13	J=2	K=7	L=12
M=11	N=8	O=1	P=14

A Streetcar Named Desire Vocabulary Magic Squares 2

Match the definition with the vocabulary word. Put your answers in the magic squares below. When your answers are correct, all columns and rows will add to the same number.

A. TRANQUILITY
B. UNCOUTH
C. GAUDY
D. COSMOPOLITAN
E. HOARSELY
F. EXPRESSIONS
G. VALISE
H. REVERBERATED
I. EFFEMINATE
J. SINISTER
K. COMMON
L. BASHFUL
M. INDIFFERENCE
N. GROTESQUE
O. EXHILARATION
P. HETEROGENEOUS

1. Sayings
2. Feminine
3. Feeling of stimulation
4. Worldly
5. Lack of concern
6. Crude; rough; unpolished
7. Echoed
8. Ordinary
9. Showy
10. Different
11. Evil
12. With a strained voice
13. Shy
14. Suitcase
15. Peace
16. Unnatural or ugly

A=	B=	C=	D=
E=	F=	G=	H=
I=	J=	K=	L=
M=	N=	O=	P=

A Streetcar Named Desire Vocabulary Magic Squares 2 Answer Key

Match the definition with the vocabulary word. Put your answers in the magic squares below. When your answers are correct, all columns and rows will add to the same number.

A. TRANQUILITY
B. UNCOUTH
C. GAUDY
D. COSMOPOLITAN
E. HOARSELY
F. EXPRESSIONS
G. VALISE
H. REVERBERATED
I. EFFEMINATE
J. SINISTER
K. COMMON
L. BASHFUL
M. INDIFFERENCE
N. GROTESQUE
O. EXHILARATION
P. HETEROGENEOUS

1. Sayings
2. Feminine
3. Feeling of stimulation
4. Worldly
5. Lack of concern
6. Crude; rough; unpolished
7. Echoed
8. Ordinary
9. Showy
10. Different
11. Evil
12. With a strained voice
13. Shy
14. Suitcase
15. Peace
16. Unnatural or ugly

A=15	B=6	C=9	D=4
E=12	F=1	G=14	H=7
I=2	J=11	K=8	L=13
M=5	N=16	O=3	P=10

A Streetcar Named Desire Vocabulary Magic Squares 3

Match the definition with the vocabulary word. Put your answers in the magic squares below. When your answers are correct, all columns and rows will add to the same number.

A. MALARKEY
B. DIFFIDENT
C. INEFFECTUAL
D. RAFFISH
E. DEPLETION
F. NOCTURNAL
G. SINUOUSLY
H. INDECENT
I. RETREATING
J. SUFFICIENT
K. MENACING
L. CULTIVATED
M. CLEFT
N. REPERTOIRE
O. VALISE
P. SACCHARINE

1. Improper
2. Hollowed area
3. Timid
4. Threatening
5. Enough
6. Unsatisfactory; not effective
7. Overly sweet
8. Scarcity
9. Suitcase
10. During darkness
11. Going backwards
12. Vulgar
13. Foolish talk
14. Tended
15. Curving or twisting
16. Collection

A=	B=	C=	D=
E=	F=	G=	H=
I=	J=	K=	L=
M=	N=	O=	P=

A Streetcar Named Desire Vocabulary Magic Squares 3 Answer Key

Match the definition with the vocabulary word. Put your answers in the magic squares below. When your answers are correct, all columns and rows will add to the same number.

A. MALARKEY
B. DIFFIDENT
C. INEFFECTUAL
D. RAFFISH
E. DEPLETION
F. NOCTURNAL
G. SINUOUSLY
H. INDECENT
I. RETREATING
J. SUFFICIENT
K. MENACING
L. CULTIVATED
M. CLEFT
N. REPERTOIRE
O. VALISE
P. SACCHARINE

1. Improper
2. Hollowed area
3. Timid
4. Threatening
5. Enough
6. Unsatisfactory; not effective
7. Overly sweet
8. Scarcity
9. Suitcase
10. During darkness
11. Going backwards
12. Vulgar
13. Foolish talk
14. Tended
15. Curving or twisting
16. Collection

A=13	B=3	C=6	D=12
E=8	F=10	G=15	H=1
I=11	J=5	K=4	L=14
M=2	N=16	O=9	P=7

A Streetcar Named Desire Vocabulary Magic Squares 4

Match the definition with the vocabulary word. Put your answers in the magic squares below. When your answers are correct, all columns and rows will add to the same number.

A. REVERBERATED
B. PERPETUAL
C. REFLECTIVELY
D. INERT
E. SINISTER
F. IMPROVIDENT
G. COSMOPOLITAN
H. COMMON
I. MENACING
J. PERPETRATED
K. YEARNINGLY
L. PERPLEXITY
M. INDISTINGUISHABLE
N. IMMEASURABLY
O. EXTRACTION
P. EXHILARATION

1. Never ending
2. Worldly
3. With desire
4. Vast
5. Not understandable; not clear
6. Confusion or uncertainty
7. Ordinary
8. Echoed
9. Feeling of stimulation
10. Threatening
11. Evil
12. Unable to move or act
13. Thoughtfully
14. Lacking judgment
15. Committed
16. Lineage; from what people one has come

A=	B=	C=	D=
E=	F=	G=	H=
I=	J=	K=	L=
M=	N=	O=	P=

A Streetcar Named Desire Vocabulary Magic Squares 4 Answer Key

Match the definition with the vocabulary word. Put your answers in the magic squares below. When your answers are correct, all columns and rows will add to the same number.

A. REVERBERATED
B. PERPETUAL
C. REFLECTIVELY
D. INERT
E. SINISTER
F. IMPROVIDENT
G. COSMOPOLITAN
H. COMMON
I. MENACING
J. PERPETRATED
K. YEARNINGLY
L. PERPLEXITY
M. INDISTINGUISHABLE
N. IMMEASURABLY
O. EXTRACTION
P. EXHILARATION

1. Never ending
2. Worldly
3. With desire
4. Vast
5. Not understandable; not clear
6. Confusion or uncertainty
7. Ordinary
8. Echoed
9. Feeling of stimulation
10. Threatening
11. Evil
12. Unable to move or act
13. Thoughtfully
14. Lacking judgment
15. Committed
16. Lineage; from what people one has come

A=8	B=1	C=13	D=12
E=11	F=14	G=2	H=7
I=10	J=15	K=3	L=6
M=5	N=4	O=16	P=9

A Streetcar Named Desire Vocabulary Word Search 1

```
V A L I S E C V N Q M H H F C O A R S E
N D E P L E T I O N A F R E T S I N E S
P Q D W V X P V S H L P L I G A U D Y S
Q H G B H I Z A W B A U Y G P Q R J C X
F Q U X D Y V C I F R K R N R F E I W H
G J Y N K H M I N I K H O E I E T O R D
I N D E C E N T D E E D T D M C R G H T
N V Q T U H R Y L V Y F I G E N E R U C
E S I H L M E G E P E N S H A E A O M R
R P R E T V D A L D O N Y M R T T B L
T I E T I P E N C N C K A T I E I E A J
N N P E V O R D O P D C R I A F N S S L
E S R R A R B E O T Y E T X B F G Q H W
L U O O T E P L L I R R E I I T U F G
O F A G E I R L R A E O J L L D D E U Y
D F C E D E A Y C I T N N P I N M K L X
N E H N P R T D K S M E C R T I N E Z J
I R G E I E E W O P G I D E Y B V K S T
J A W O N S D L F P W T T P T A E C L Y
K B V U I B E Q B D E T B I R F X A Y N
Z L S S O M R A F F I S H G V P S X M Z
J Y K U N C O U T H L A R T C E P S N S
```

Bent over; crouched (7)
Blame (8)
Chaotic (6)
Confusion or uncertainty (10)
Crude; rough; unpolished (7)
Cuban dance (6)
Different (13)
Document of ownership (4)
Echoed (12)
Evil (8)
Fight (3)
Figure (6)
Foolish talk (8)
Friendliness (10)
Ghostly (8)
Going backwards (10)
Gossip (4)
Happy (6)
Heavy curtains (9)
Hollowed area (5)
Horrible (5)
Idea (6)
Improper (8)
Intense (5)
Lack of concern (12)
Lazy (8)

Like early mankind (9)
Liveliness (8)
Look (6)
Natural; unprocessed (6)
Odor; fragrance (9)
Pretended (7)
Radiates (5)
Scam (7)
Scarcity (9)
Serious (6)
Seriously (7)
Set talk designed to persuade (5)
Showy (5)
Shy (7)
Stiffly proper or precise in manner or
  appearance (4)
Suitcase (6)
Temporary (10)
Tended (10)
Unable to move or act (5)
Unbearably (12)
Unnatural or ugly (9)
Vulgar (7)
Wrestle; hold down (6)

A Streetcar Named Desire Vocablar Word Search 1 Answer Key

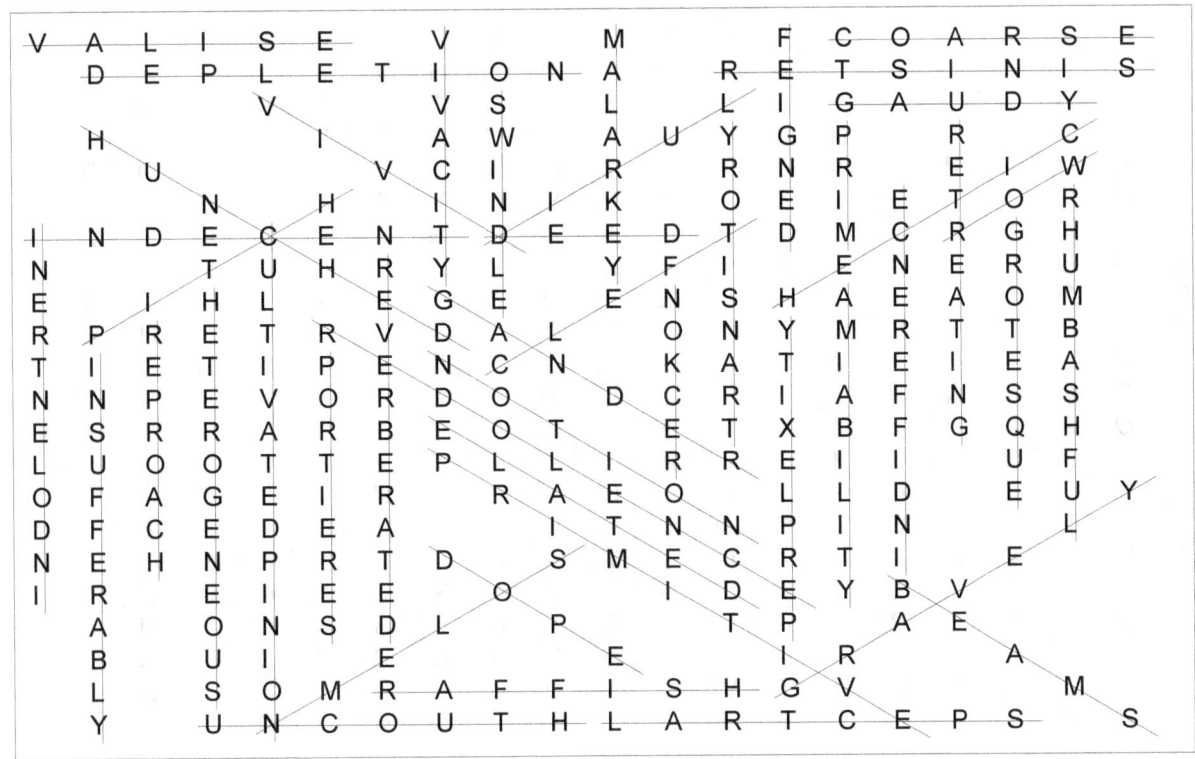

AMIABILITY	HUNCHED	REDOLENCE
BASHFUL	INDECENT	REPROACH
BEAMS	INDIFFERENCE	RETREATING
CLEFT	INDOLENT	REVERBERATED
COARSE	INERT	RHUMBA
CULTIVATED	INSUFFERABLY	ROW
DEED	LURID	SINISTER
DEPLETION	MALARKEY	SOLEMN
DOPE	NOTION	SPECTRAL
ELATED	PERPLEXITY	SWINDLE
FEIGNED	PINION	TRANSITORY
GANDER	PITCH	UNCOUTH
GAUDY	PORTIERES	VALISE
GRAVELY	PRIM	VIVACITY
GROTESQUE	PRIMITIVE	VIVID
HECTIC	RAFFISH	
HETEROGENEOUS	RECKON	

A Streetcar Named Desire Vocabulary Word Search 2

```
B L A P P I N G Q R C Y R G N Q Z H C M
E G R I I B U X E G L Q D S W B Y U A X
A I H N T N E D G S E I H O K E W N L X
M P L C C I N S U F F E R A B L Y C L J
S M I O H A N O T F T E A Z W L T H O G
L M U N G P U N I I P R F N G O I E U X
I T K G I T X D P R A Y F N H W U D S W
H N G R P O E P O D D L I R E I Q P M S
N H D U R N N A R E F N S Z T N I R E K
G R L O T L C P T T R O H R E G T O N R
H O C U L H M S I A W I V E R H N D A K
V O O S X E E B E L L T A P O E A I C Z
X Q A L R V N Y R E A E L E G C T G I J
K I R R I Y H T E R N L I R E T I I N Z
D N S D S L G J S E R P S T N I L O G N
V E E W I E Y N O C U E E O E C O U T J
R R E Q N N L J L K T D I I O J P S C B
H T V D I E U Y E O C T P R U K O L O B
U M I G S R R R M N O X Q E S B M Y M W
M P V Q T E I K N N G A U D Y S P M Z
B X I N E S D S W I N D L E D J O L O F
A R D T R E X T R A C T I O N B C M N X
```

Ancient times (9)
Bent over; crouched (7)
Blame (8)
Calmly (8)
Chaotic (6)
Collection (10)
Crude; rough; unpolished (7)
Cuban dance (6)
Different (13)
Document of ownership (4)
Drinking up, like a dog (7)
During darkness (9)
Evil (8)
Fight (3)
Figure (6)
Gossip (4)
Got rid of (8)
Happy (6)
Heavy curtains (9)
Hollowed area (5)
Horrible (5)
Idea (6)
Inhuman (7)
Insensitive (7)
Intense (5)
Lazy (8)

Lineage; from what people one has come (10)
Look (6)
Natural; unprocessed (6)
Ordinary (6)
Out of place (11)
Radiates (5)
Roaring (9)
Scam (7)
Scarcity (9)
Sensuously (12)
Serious (6)
Set talk designed to persuade (5)
Showy (5)
Stiffly proper or precise in manner or appearance (4)
Suitcase (6)
Threatening (8)
Timid (9)
Unable to move or act (5)
Unbearably (12)
Vulgar (7)
With a strained voice (8)
With desire (10)
Wonderfully (12)
Worldly (12)
Wrestle; hold down (6)

A Streetcar Named Desire Vocablar Word Search 2 Answer Key

```
B L A P P I N G   R C Y           H C
E   R I B U   E     L   D   W   B U A
A   I N T N E D   S E I     O   E N L
M P   C C I N S U F F E R A B L Y N L
S   I O H A   O T F T E A       L T O
    U N G   U   I I P   F       G I U
I T   G I T   D P R A   F N   H O U S
H N   R P O E P O D D   L I   E H W M
      D U N   N A R E   N S   T   I E
      L T   C   T T R   O H   E   N N
H   O C U L H   S I A   I V   R   G A
V O O S   E   E   E L   T A   O   H C
  O A S   V N Y T R A   E L   G   E I
  I R R   Y   R E N L   R I   E   A N
D N S E D L     S R P I T S   N   T G
  E E   I     T O C U E O E   E   I
R R E   N     Y L K T D I R   O   L C
H   V D S     E M O C T R E   U   O O
U   I I T     R N O   I S     S   P M
M   V   E       N N G A U D Y M   S M
B   I   R     S W I N D L E       O O
A   D   E X T R A C T I O N       C N
```

ANTIQUITY
BEAMS
BELLOWING
BESTIAL
CALLOUS
CLEFT
COARSE
COMMON
COSMOPOLITAN
DEED
DEPLETION
DIFFIDENT
DIVESTED
DOPE
ELATED
EXTRACTION
GANDER

GAUDY
HECTIC
HETEROGENEOUS
HOARSELY
HUNCHED
INCONGRUOUS
INDOLENT
INERT
INSUFFERABLY
LAPPING
LURID
MENACING
NOCTURNAL
NOTION
PINION
PITCH
PORTIERES

PRIM
PRODIGIOUSLY
RAFFISH
RECKON
REPERTOIRE
REPROACH
RHUMBA
ROW
SERENELY
SINISTER
SOLEMN
SWINDLE
UNCOUTH
VALISE
VIVID
VOLUPTUOUSLY
YEARNINGLY

A Streetcar Named Desire Vocablar Word Search 3

```
C O M M O N X E F F E M I N A T E B D M
Q O X V F D S C A L L O U S L N L E C J
Q R A N Q I K N P M M S A R E A L D J Y
C E W R L Z S E Z K W Q T U E C P L J T
Q C V A S M G L F I B N Y N P E P O P N
F K V I A E Y O N F E M L C R D I W T R
K O R E V M J D X M S E S O O N N I H F
E N B J J A L E A G T L U U A I G N U I
U R T L P E C R S A I O O T C H L G N N
Q Y H V R H E I N U A S I H H E U E C G
S T D U I P O L T D L G D S C R Y H H
E I K C M H X A A Y P R I M I T I V E V
T X L E C B G B R T M V D F F I D C D P
O E T T H R A O A S E H O Z F C H H Q D
R L I W C W T W N S E D R C A I Q S O S
G P L Z O I J F T K H L P T R N D P H F
V R R R S R N E F G Y F Y H O D E E F K
J E A N K O D I E V A X U I W O S C N V
X P A V I F J G L I R N N L J L D T D T
P R Y T E N T N C V L I D D E E D R H F
T W O R W L P E T I P T C E T N D A Y G
N N X D F T Y D V D K X B F R T R L S G
```

BASHFUL
BEAMS
BELLOWING
BESTIAL
CALLOUS
CLEFT
COARSE
COMMON
DEED
DIFFIDENT
DIVESTED
DOPE
EFFEMINATE
ELATED
FEIGNED
GANDER
GAUDY

GRAVELY
GROTESQUE
HECTIC
HOARSELY
HUNCHED
INDECENT
INDOLENT
INERT
LAPPING
LURID
NOTION
PERPLEXITY
PINION
PITCH
PRIM
PRIMITIVE
PRODIGIOUSLY

RAFFISH
RECKON
REDOLENCE
REPROACH
RHUMBA
ROW
SOLEMN
SPECTRAL
SWINDLE
TEMPERAMENTAL
TRANSITORY
UNCOUTH
VALISE
VIVACITY
VIVID

A Streetcar Named Desire Vocablar Word Search 3 Answer Key

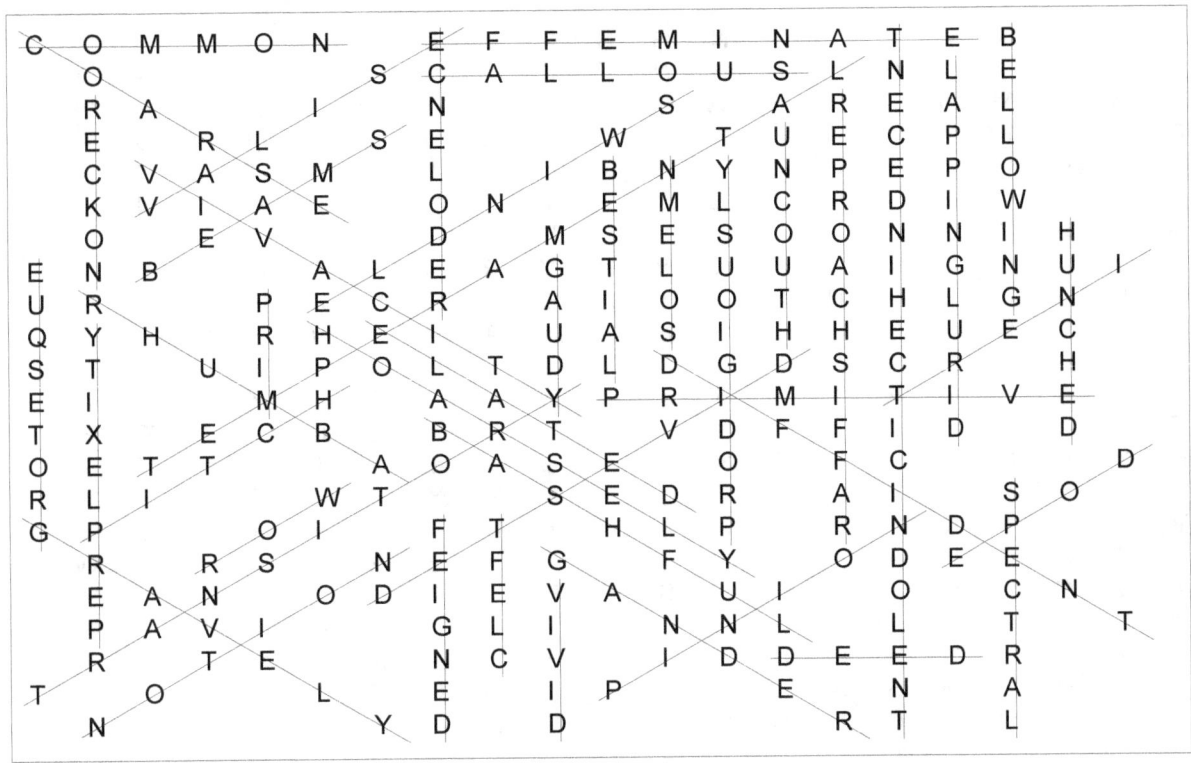

BASHFUL	GRAVELY	RAFFISH
BEAMS	GROTESQUE	RECKON
BELLOWING	HECTIC	REDOLENCE
BESTIAL	HOARSELY	REPROACH
CALLOUS	HUNCHED	RHUMBA
CLEFT	INDECENT	ROW
COARSE	INDOLENT	SOLEMN
COMMON	INERT	SPECTRAL
DEED	LAPPING	SWINDLE
DIFFIDENT	LURID	TEMPERAMENTAL
DIVESTED	NOTION	TRANSITORY
DOPE	PERPLEXITY	UNCOUTH
EFFEMINATE	PINION	VALISE
ELATED	PITCH	VIVACITY
FEIGNED	PRIM	VIVID
GANDER	PRIMITIVE	
GAUDY	PRODIGIOUSLY	

A Streetcar Named Desire Vocablar Word Search 4

```
R E T R E A T I N G S P E C T R A L G B
E L F N J E N R B N R I Q L O J F Y A Q
L A X M O X E E W I T S N A W M L F U L
D T Q E Y T D P J P E N O C R M N D P
N E C L Z R I R L P M C T O H V O Y M
I D Y O H A F O G A P T E A U Z L N S
W W E S Z C F A N L E I U P R M S T Y D
S M A U S T I C X M R U R R S B Z L T R
E G R F H I D H A Y A E N E E A E N T P
R X N F G O Z L R L M N P V V E D N K
E C I I M N A O L D E T L H I C V E H R
N L N C G R T R B J N A S T E H H T H C
E E G I K I E P S N T L C D C C F A T B
L F L E S D N D R E A N M G T T V U S
Y T Y N A M I A B I L I T Y P I N I O N
V T A K V R V F F M Y F V N P N T C L
V R Z B I B A L E W R D R E A D L L N W
T V G V R E H R I S C E R O O L D U U P
W D E E D A C D G F T T C L W I I C Y S
Y J O T S M C F N R L E E K R L X S D S
P C M P M S A Z E C W N D U O Z Q M E Q
K J Z Q E G S H D S T B L G A N D E R M
```

AMIABILITY	INDECENT	ROW
BEAMS	INDOLENT	SACCHARINE
CLEFT	INERT	SENTIMENTAL
COARSE	LAPPING	SERENELY
COMMON	LURID	SINUOUSLY
CULTIVATED	MALARKEY	SOLEMN
DEED	NOCTURNAL	SPECTRAL
DIFFIDENT	NOTION	SUFFICIENT
DIVESTED	PERPETUAL	SWINDLE
DOPE	PINION	TEMPERAMENTAL
ELATED	PITCH	TRANSITORY
EXTRACTION	PRIM	UNCOUTH
FEIGNED	RECKON	VALISE
GANDER	REFLECTIVELY	VIVID
GAUDY	REPROACH	YEARNINGLY
HECTIC	RETREATING	
HOARSELY	RHUMBA	

A Streetcar Named Desire Vocablar Word Search 4 Answer Key

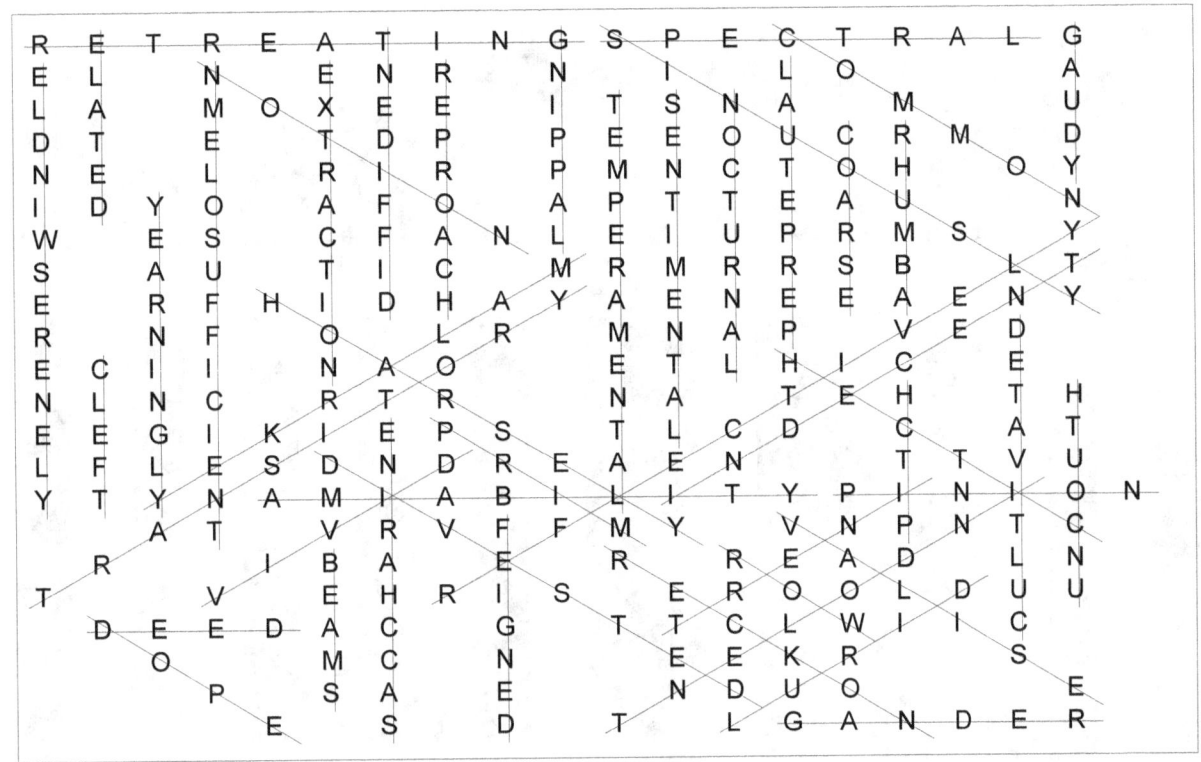

AMIABILITY
BEAMS
CLEFT
COARSE
COMMON
CULTIVATED
DEED
DIFFIDENT
DIVESTED
DOPE
ELATED
EXTRACTION
FEIGNED
GANDER
GAUDY
HECTIC
HOARSELY

INDECENT
INDOLENT
INERT
LAPPING
LURID
MALARKEY
NOCTURNAL
NOTION
PERPETUAL
PINION
PITCH
PRIM
RECKON
REFLECTIVELY
REPROACH
RETREATING
RHUMBA

ROW
SACCHARINE
SENTIMENTAL
SERENELY
SINUOUSLY
SOLEMN
SPECTRAL
SUFFICIENT
SWINDLE
TEMPERAMENTAL
TRANSITORY
UNCOUTH
VALISE
VIVID
YEARNINGLY

A Streetcar Named Desire Vocabulary Crossword 1

Across
2. Improper
4. Delicate fabric
6. Fight
8. Bent over; crouched
10. Temporary
13. Gossip
15. Document of ownership
17. Crude; rough; unpolished
18. Hollowed area
20. Emotional
21. Pretended
22. Vulgar

Down
1. Horrible
3. Tended
4. Look
5. Lineage; from what people one has come
7. Shy
8. Chaotic
9. Sayings
11. Serious
12. Odor; fragrance
14. Threateningly
15. Scarcity
16. Set talk designed to persuade
19. Radiates

A Streetcar Named Desire Vocabulary Crossword 1 Answer Key

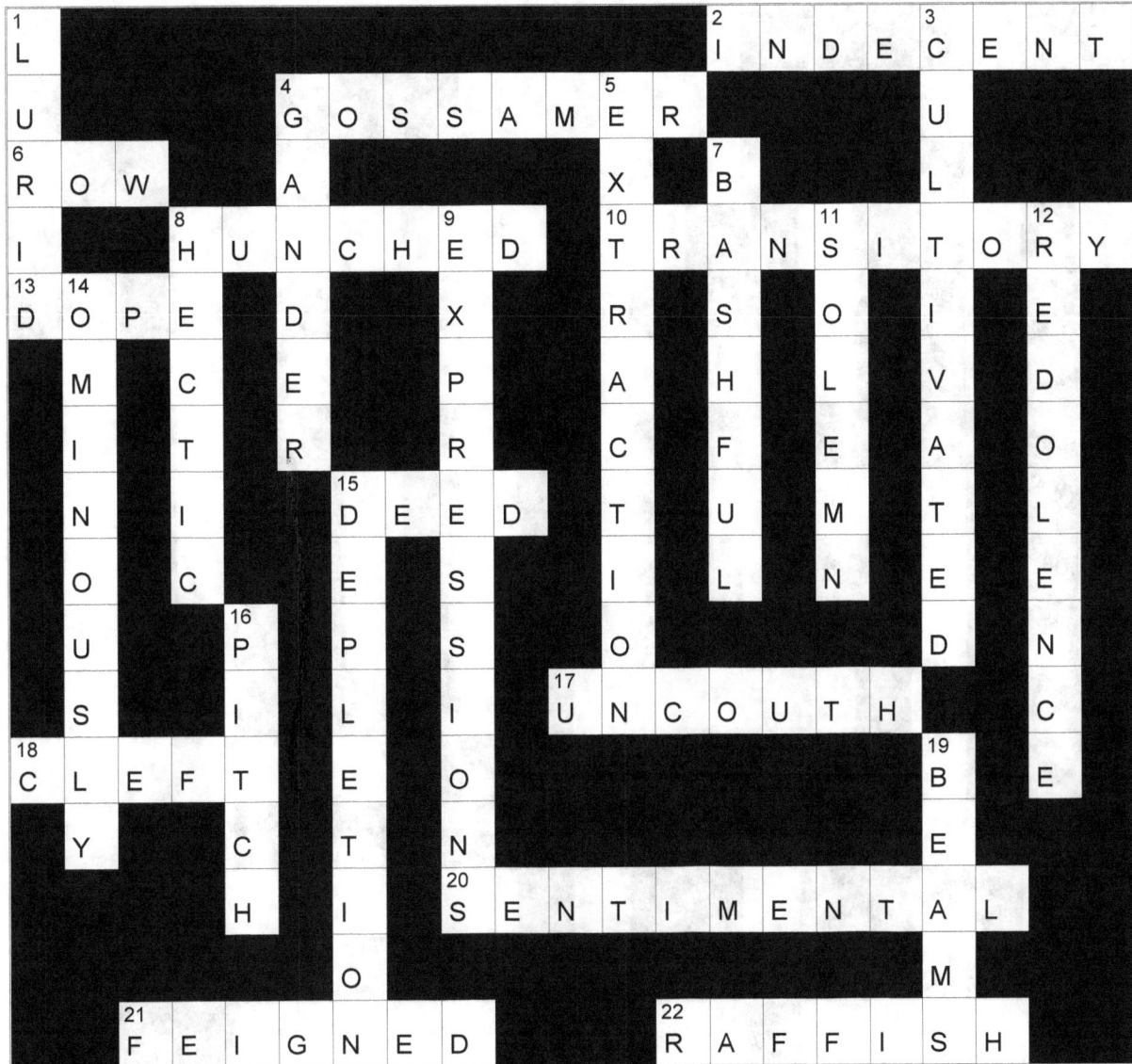

Across
- 2. Improper
- 4. Delicate fabric
- 6. Fight
- 8. Bent over; crouched
- 10. Temporary
- 13. Gossip
- 15. Document of ownership
- 17. Crude; rough; unpolished
- 18. Hollowed area
- 20. Emotional
- 21. Pretended
- 22. Vulgar

Down
- 1. Horrible
- 3. Tended
- 4. Look
- 5. Lineage; from what people one has come
- 7. Shy
- 8. Chaotic
- 9. Sayings
- 11. Serious
- 12. Odor; fragrance
- 14. Threateningly
- 15. Scarcity
- 16. Set talk designed to persuade
- 19. Radiates

A Streetcar Named Desire Vocabulary Crossword 2

Across
3. Wonderfully
7. Like early mankind
10. With desire
13. Stiffly proper or precise in manner or appearance
14. Hollowed area
15. Set talk designed to persuade
17. Scam
18. Document of ownership
19. Inhuman
20. Figure
21. During darkness

Down
1. Ordinary
2. Fight
3. Never ending
4. Showy
5. Calmly
6. Unpredictable; not consistent
8. Threatening
9. Curving or twisting
11. Feminine
12. Horrible
14. Natural; unprocessed
16. Chaotic
18. Gossip

A Streetcar Named Desire Vocabulary Crossword 2 Answer Key

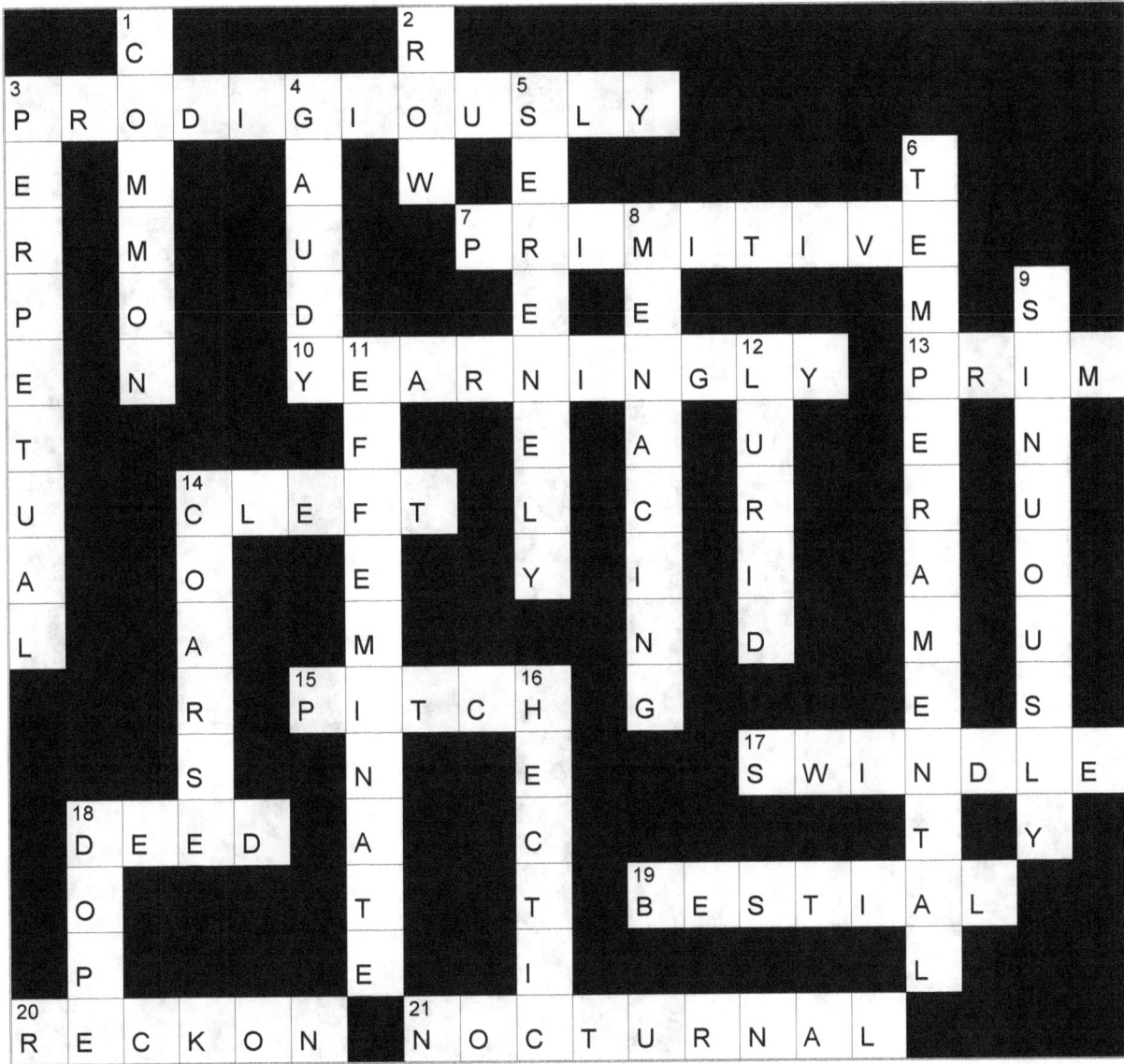

Across
3. Wonderfully
7. Like early mankind
10. With desire
13. Stiffly proper or precise in manner or appearance
14. Hollowed area
15. Set talk designed to persuade
17. Scam
18. Document of ownership
19. Inhuman
20. Figure
21. During darkness

Down
1. Ordinary
2. Fight
3. Never ending
4. Showy
5. Calmly
6. Unpredictable; not consistent
8. Threatening
9. Curving or twisting
11. Feminine
12. Horrible
14. Natural; unprocessed
16. Chaotic
18. Gossip

A Streetcar Named Desire Vocabulary Crossword 3

Across
1. Horrible
4. During darkness
7. Modesty
8. Seriously
10. Feeling of stimulation
14. Fight
15. Inhuman
18. Ancient times
19. Happy
20. Stiffly proper or precise in manner or appearance
21. Ghostly

Down
2. Discourteous
3. Improper
5. Unpredictable; not consistent
6. Delicate fabric
7. Scarcity
8. Unnatural or ugly
9. Serious
11. Chaotic
12. Temporary
13. Wrestle; hold down
15. Radiates
16. Unable to move or act
17. Document of ownership

A Streetcar Named Desire Vocabulary Crossword 3 Answer Key

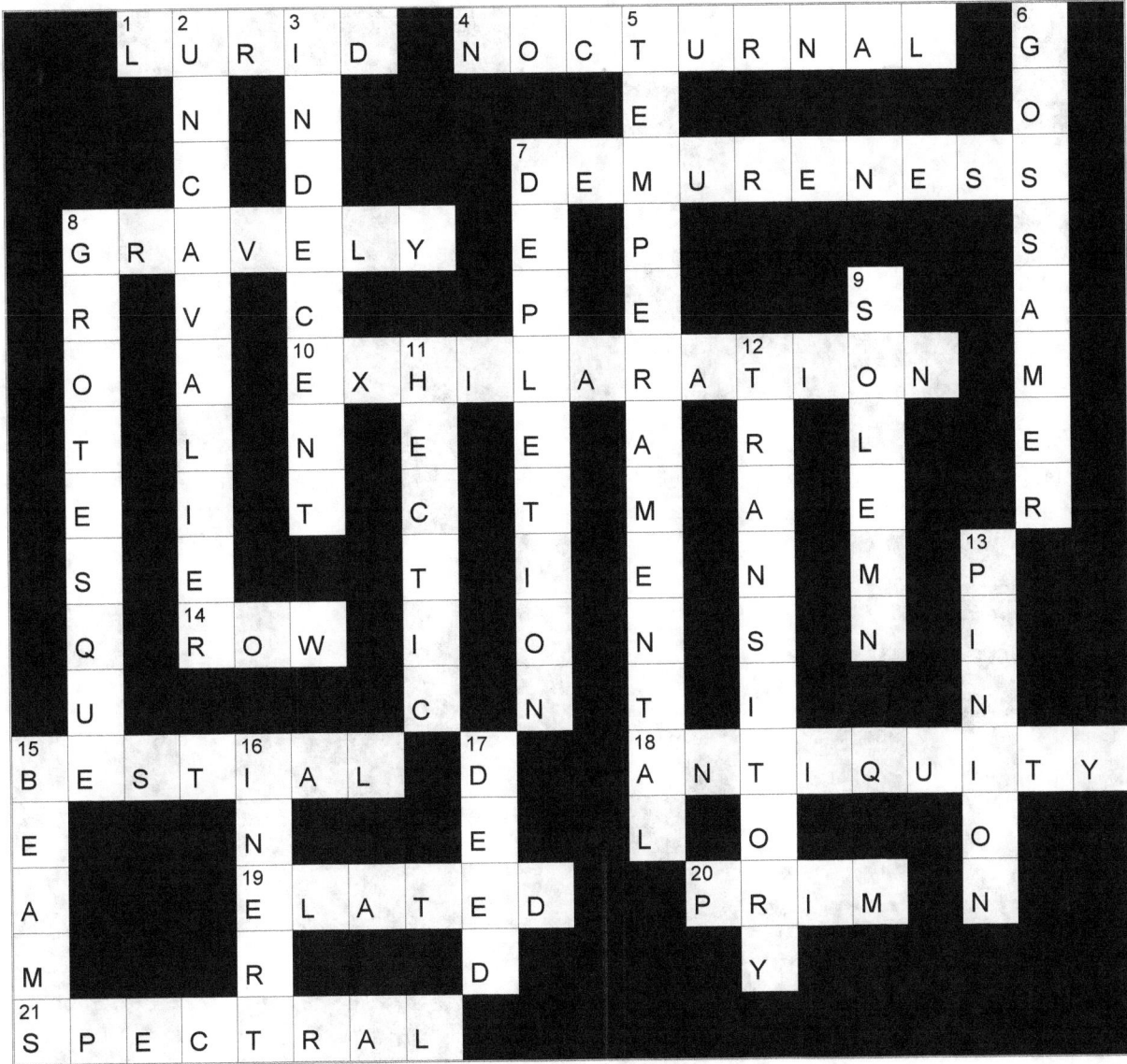

Across
1. Horrible
4. During darkness
7. Modesty
8. Seriously
10. Feeling of stimulation
14. Fight
15. Inhuman
18. Ancient times
19. Happy
20. Stiffly proper or precise in manner or appearance
21. Ghostly

Down
2. Discourteous
3. Improper
5. Unpredictable; not consistent
6. Delicate fabric
7. Scarcity
8. Unnatural or ugly
9. Serious
11. Chaotic
12. Temporary
13. Wrestle; hold down
15. Radiates
16. Unable to move or act
17. Document of ownership

A Streetcar Named Desire Vocabulary Crossword 4

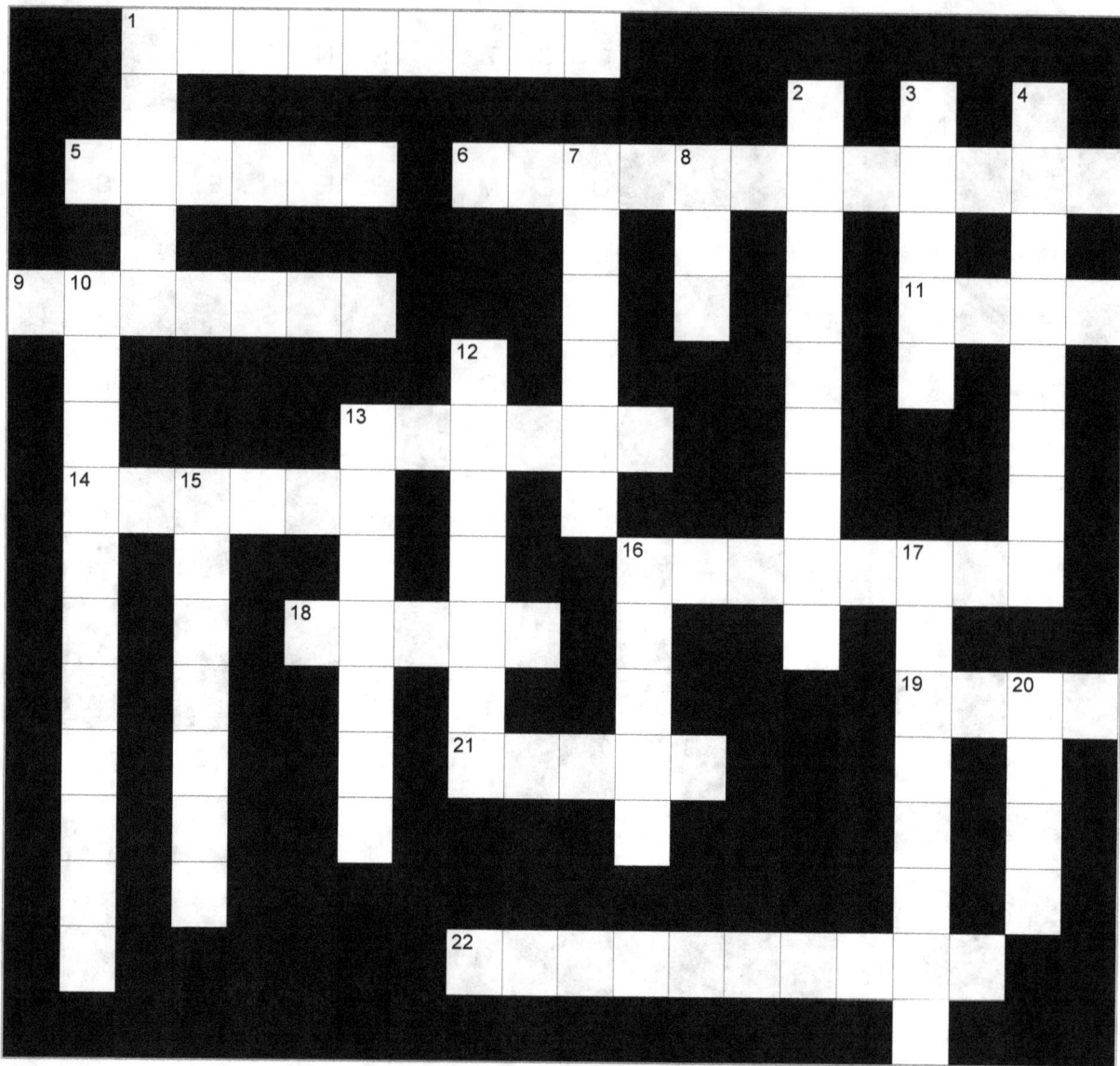

Across
1. Roaring
5. Look
6. Echoed
9. Inhuman
11. Document of ownership
13. Natural; unprocessed
14. Cuban dance
16. Liveliness
18. Hollowed area
19. Gossip
21. Horrible
22. Going backwards

Down
1. Radiates
2. Never ending
3. Showy
4. Calmly
7. Suitcase
8. Fight
10. Sayings
12. Shy
13. Insensitive
15. Crude; rough; unpolished
16. Intense
17. Lazy
20. Stiffly proper or precise in manner or appearance

A Streetcar Named Desire Vocabulary Crossword 4 Answer Key

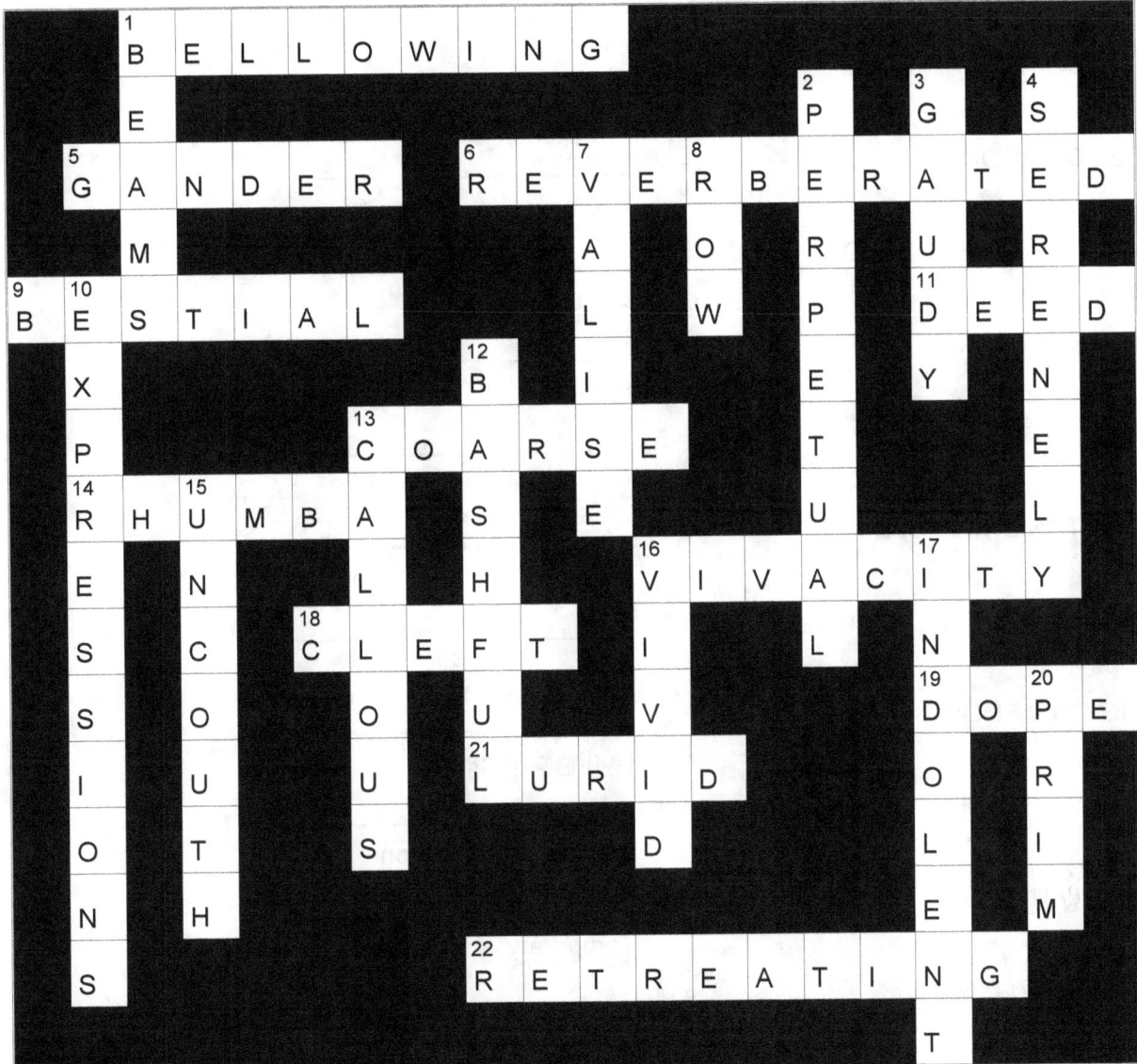

Across
1. Roaring
5. Look
6. Echoed
9. Inhuman
11. Document of ownership
13. Natural; unprocessed
14. Cuban dance
16. Liveliness
18. Hollowed area
19. Gossip
21. Horrible
22. Going backwards

Down
1. Radiates
2. Never ending
3. Showy
4. Calmly
7. Suitcase
8. Fight
10. Sayings
12. Shy
13. Insensitive
15. Crude; rough; unpolished
16. Intense
17. Lazy
20. Stiffly proper or precise in manner or appearance

A Streetcar Named Desire Vocabulary Juggle Letters 1

1. DOLTIENPE = 1. _____
   Scarcity

2. OMMCON = 2. _____
   Ordinary

3. EGEHEUENOSTRO = 3. _____
   Different

4. NMEEFFAEIT = 4. _____
   Feminine

5. EDESTUTTI = 5. _____
   Without necessities; poor

6. ITDNIBNSUAGLESHII = 6. _____
   Not understandable; not clear

7. INSERIST = 7. _____
   Evil

8. RNLATNOUC = 8. _____
   During darkness

9. AXLRTENHIIAO = 9. _____
   Feeling of stimulation

10. RYTNRTISAO = 10. _____
    Temporary

11. GERYLIYNAN = 11. _____
    With desire

12. ARHMBU = 12. _____
    Cuban dance

13. ODPE = 13. _____
    Gossip

14. FDEIIEENNRCF = 14. _____
    Lack of concern

A Streetcar Named Desire Vocabulary Juggle Letters 1 Answer Key

1. DOLTIENPE = 1. DEPLETION
   Scarcity

2. OMMCON = 2. COMMON
   Ordinary

3. EGEHEUENOSTRO = 3. HETEROGENEOUS
   Different

4. NMEEFFAEIT = 4. EFFEMINATE
   Feminine

5. EDESTUTTI = 5. DESTITUTE
   Without necessities; poor

6. ITDNIBNSUAGLESHII = 6. INDISTINGUISHABLE
   Not understandable; not clear

7. INSERIST = 7. SINISTER
   Evil

8. RNLATNOUC = 8. NOCTURNAL
   During darkness

9. AXLRTENHIIAO = 9. EXHILARATION
   Feeling of stimulation

10. RYTNRTISAO =10. TRANSITORY
    Temporary

11. GERYLIYNAN =11. YEARNINGLY
    With desire

12. ARHMBU =12. RHUMBA
    Cuban dance

13. ODPE =13. DOPE
    Gossip

14. FDEIIEENNRCF =14. INDIFFERENCE
    Lack of concern

A Streetcar Named Desire Vocabulary Juggle Letters 2

1. RCNUSGIONUO = 1. _____
   Out of place

2. TEEDRTPPEAR = 2. _____
   Committed

3. ITEMVPIRI = 3. _____
   Like early mankind

4. HTIPC = 4. _____
   Set talk designed to persuade

5. RAEEEEBVRTDR = 5. _____
   Echoed

6. EEYLERNS = 6. _____
   Calmly

7. LBNLIEGWO = 7. _____
   Roaring

8. EERYPXTLPI = 8. _____
   Confusion or uncertainty

9. IALEVS = 9. _____
   Suitcase

10. CANIEMGN =10. _____
    Threatening

11. BMUHRA =11. _____
    Cuban dance

12. OLNPETEID =12. _____
    Scarcity

13. DCITENNE =13. _____
    Improper

14. LAEEDT =14. _____
    Happy

A Streetcar Named Desire Vocabulary Juggle Letters 2 Answer Key

1. RCNUSGIONUO = 1. INCONGRUOUS
   Out of place

2. TEEDRTPPEAR = 2. PERPETRATED
   Committed

3. ITEMVPIRI = 3. PRIMITIVE
   Like early mankind

4. HTIPC = 4. PITCH
   Set talk designed to persuade

5. RAEEEEBVRTDR = 5. REVERBERATED
   Echoed

6. EEYLERNS = 6. SERENELY
   Calmly

7. LBNLIEGWO = 7. BELLOWING
   Roaring

8. EERYPXTLPI = 8. PERPLEXITY
   Confusion or uncertainty

9. IALEVS = 9. VALISE
   Suitcase

10. CANIEMGN = 10. MENACING
    Threatening

11. BMUHRA = 11. RHUMBA
    Cuban dance

12. OLNPETEID = 12. DEPLETION
    Scarcity

13. DCITENNE = 13. INDECENT
    Improper

14. LAEEDT = 14. ELATED
    Happy

A Streetcar Named Desire Vocabulary Juggle Letters 3

1. RIOSXSEPSNE = 1. _____
   Sayings

2. OSNOCLAIOPTM = 2. _____
   Worldly

3. AIIXTALNEROH = 3. _____
   Feeling of stimulation

4. EIRNT = 4. _____
   Unable to move or act

5. TRVAEREEEBRD = 5. _____
   Echoed

6. RORESEITP = 6. _____
   Heavy curtains

7. IRLDU = 7. _____
   Horrible

8. EOTEEIRRRP = 8. _____
   Collection

9. LUEVNCAIAR = 9. _____
   Discourteous

10. NOCKER =10. _____
    Figure

11. CCSARNEIAH =11. _____
    Overly sweet

12. PTLUVOYOSULU =12. _____
    Sensuously

13. TIINESRS =13. _____
    Evil

14. TEUSGEQRO =14. _____
    Unnatural or ugly

A Streetcar Named Desire Vocabulary Juggle Letters 3 Answer Key

1. RIOSXSEPSNE = 1. EXPRESSIONS
   Sayings

2. OSNOCLAIOPTM = 2. COSMOPOLITAN
   Worldly

3. AIIXTALNEROH = 3. EXHILARATION
   Feeling of stimulation

4. EIRNT = 4. INERT
   Unable to move or act

5. TRVAEREEEBRD = 5. REVERBERATED
   Echoed

6. RORESEITP = 6. PORTIERES
   Heavy curtains

7. IRLDU = 7. LURID
   Horrible

8. EOTEEIRRRP = 8. REPERTOIRE
   Collection

9. LUEVNCAIAR = 9. UNCAVALIER
   Discourteous

10. NOCKER = 10. RECKON
    Figure

11. CCSARNEIAH = 11. SACCHARINE
    Overly sweet

12. PTLUVOYOSULU = 12. VOLUPTUOUSLY
    Sensuously

13. TIINESRS = 13. SINISTER
    Evil

14. TEUSGEQRO = 14. GROTESQUE
    Unnatural or ugly

A Streetcar Named Desire Vocabulary Juggle Letters 4

1. PRETUPALE = 1. _____
Never ending

2. YAIRNRSOTT = 2. _____
Temporary

3. MEEEANARTMPTL = 3. _____
Unpredictable; not consistent

4. AMLIYAMBURES = 4. _____
Vast

5. NOOCRGUNUSI = 5. _____
Out of place

6. OLIODYSURPIG = 6. _____
Wonderfully

7. BLISAET = 7. _____
Inhuman

8. LVFETEIYLERC = 8. _____
Thoughtfully

9. ODIRENTPVMI = 9. _____
Lacking judgment

10. FMEEFEIANT =10. _____
Feminine

11. OUSTEEQGR =11. _____
Unnatural or ugly

12. DETEREVREABR =12. _____
Echoed

13. ISNSEERSPOX =13. _____
Sayings

14. ATURNCNOL =14. _____
During darkness

A Streetcar Named Desire Vocabulary Juggle Letters 4 Answer Key

1. PRETUPALE = 1. PERPETUAL
Never ending

2. YAIRNRSOTT = 2. TRANSITORY
Temporary

3. MEEEANARTMPTL = 3. TEMPERAMENTAL
Unpredictable; not consistent

4. AMLIYAMBURES = 4. IMMEASURABLY
Vast

5. NOOCRGUNUSI = 5. INCONGRUOUS
Out of place

6. OLIODYSURPIG = 6. PRODIGIOUSLY
Wonderfully

7. BLISAET = 7. BESTIAL
Inhuman

8. LVFETEIYLERC = 8. REFLECTIVELY
Thoughtfully

9. ODIRENTPVMI = 9. IMPROVIDENT
Lacking judgment

10. FMEEFEIANT = 10. EFFEMINATE
Feminine

11. OUSTEEQGR = 11. GROTESQUE
Unnatural or ugly

12. DETEREVREABR = 12. REVERBERATED
Echoed

13. ISNSEERSPOX = 13. EXPRESSIONS
Sayings

14. ATURNCNOL = 14. NOCTURNAL
During darkness

AMIABILITY	Friendliness
ANTIQUITY	Ancient times
BASHFUL	Shy
BEAMS	Radiates
BELLOWING	Roaring

BESTIAL	Inhuman
CALLOUS	Insensitive
CLEFT	Hollowed area
COARSE	Natural; unprocessed
COMMON	Ordinary

COSMOPOLITAN	Worldly
CULTIVATED	Tended
DEED	Document of ownership
DEMURENESS	Modesty
DEPLETION	Scarcity

DESTITUTE	Without necessities; poor
DIFFIDENT	Timid
DIVESTED	Got rid of
DOPE	Gossip
EFFEMINATE	Feminine

ELATED	Happy
EXHILARATION	Feeling of stimulation
EXPRESSIONS	Sayings
EXTRACTION	Lineage; from what people one has come
FEIGNED	Pretended

GANDER	Look
GAUDY	Showy
GOSSAMER	Delicate fabric
GRAVELY	Seriously
GROTESQUE	Unnatural or ugly

HECTIC	Chaotic
HETEROGENEOUS	Different
HOARSELY	With a strained voice
HUNCHED	Bent over; crouched
IMMEASURABLY	Vast

IMPROVIDENT	Lacking judgment
INCONGRUOUS	Out of place
INDECENT	Improper
INDIFFERENCE	Lack of concern
INDISTINGUISHABLE	Not understandable; not clear

INDOLENT	Lazy
INEFFECTUAL	Unsatisfactory; not effective
INERT	Unable to move or act
INSUFFERABLY	Unbearably
LAPPING	Drinking up, like a dog

LURID	Horrible
MALARKEY	Foolish talk
MENACING	Threatening
NOCTURNAL	During darkness
NOTION	Idea

OMINOUSLY	Threateningly
PERPETRATED	Committed
PERPETUAL	Never ending
PERPLEXITY	Confusion or uncertainty
PINION	Wrestle; hold down

PITCH	Set talk designed to persuade
PORTIERES	Heavy curtains
PRIM	Stiffly proper or precise in manner or appearance
PRIMITIVE	Like early mankind
PRODIGIOUSLY	Wonderfully

RAFFISH	Vulgar
RECKON	Figure
REDOLENCE	Odor; fragrance
REFLECTIVELY	Thoughtfully
REPERTOIRE	Collection

REPROACH	Blame
RETREATING	Going backwards
REVERBERATED	Echoed
RHUMBA	Cuban dance
ROW	Fight

SACCHARINE	Overly sweet
SENTIMENTAL	Emotional
SERENELY	Calmly
SINISTER	Evil
SINUOUSLY	Curving or twisting

SOLEMN	Serious
SPECTRAL	Ghostly
SUFFICIENT	Enough
SWINDLE	Scam
TEMPERAMENTAL	Unpredictable; not consistent

TRANQUILITY	Peace
TRANSITORY	Temporary
UNCAVALIER	Discourteous
UNCOUTH	Crude; rough; unpolished
VALISE	Suitcase

VIVACITY	Liveliness
VIVID	Intense
VOLUPTUOUSLY	Sensuously
YEARNINGLY	With desire

A Streetcar Named Desire Vocab

GANDER	TEMPERAMENTAL	SERENELY	NOTION	SINISTER
GROTESQUE	REDOLENCE	PERPETUAL	DIVESTED	TRANSITORY
PITCH	BEAMS	FREE SPACE	EXHILARATION	AMIABILITY
NOCTURNAL	BESTIAL	ROW	ELATED	GAUDY
HECTIC	COMMON	COARSE	UNCOUTH	VIVID

A Streetcar Named Desire Vocab

INCONGRUOUS	INSUFFERABLY	REPROACH	BELLOWING	COSMOPOLITAN
CULTIVATED	DEPLETION	IMPROVIDENT	BASHFUL	SOLEMN
LURID	VIVACITY	FREE SPACE	REPERTOIRE	HUNCHED
SINUOUSLY	DESTITUTE	REFLECTIVELY	SPECTRAL	INDISTINGUISHABLE
EFFEMINATE	VALISE	INERT	PRIM	DEMURENESS

A Streetcar Named Desire Vocab

EXTRACTION	DIVESTED	OMINOUSLY	INDECENT	VIVACITY
LURID	PRODIGIOUSLY	PRIM	SINISTER	SENTIMENTAL
BASHFUL	INCONGRUOUS	FREE SPACE	HOARSELY	PERPETUAL
COSMOPOLITAN	EXPRESSIONS	DOPE	RHUMBA	SACCHARINE
GAUDY	FEIGNED	GRAVELY	YEARNINGLY	IMMEASURABLY

A Streetcar Named Desire Vocab

DESTITUTE	GOSSAMER	GANDER	DEED	CALLOUS
LAPPING	PINION	COMMON	RAFFISH	SERENELY
MALARKEY	VALISE	FREE SPACE	UNCOUTH	PERPETRATED
EXHILARATION	SPECTRAL	PERPLEXITY	INDIFFERENCE	MENACING
REVERBERATED	SOLEMN	CULTIVATED	REPERTOIRE	NOCTURNAL

A Streetcar Named Desire Vocab

GAUDY	INCONGRUOUS	INSUFFERABLY	GRAVELY	REPROACH
TRANQUILITY	RAFFISH	VIVID	REDOLENCE	NOCTURNAL
GOSSAMER	GANDER	FREE SPACE	RHUMBA	ROW
IMPROVIDENT	DEMURENESS	VIVACITY	HUNCHED	BEAMS
RETREATING	EFFEMINATE	REVERBERATED	BESTIAL	PERPETUAL

A Streetcar Named Desire Vocab

HOARSELY	PERPLEXITY	VALISE	REPERTOIRE	AMIABILITY
ANTIQUITY	COMMON	LAPPING	TRANSITORY	PERPETRATED
FEIGNED	YEARNINGLY	FREE SPACE	INERT	TEMPERAMENTAL
DESTITUTE	INDECENT	SINUOUSLY	INDOLENT	CLEFT
PRIM	EXTRACTION	MALARKEY	DIVESTED	SUFFICIENT

A Streetcar Named Desire Vocab

PRIM	ELATED	CULTIVATED	REDOLENCE	HOARSELY
CALLOUS	EXHILARATION	GRAVELY	FEIGNED	YEARNINGLY
SACCHARINE	INDISTINGUISHABLE	FREE SPACE	RHUMBA	INDIFFERENCE
IMPROVIDENT	PORTIERES	GROTESQUE	REVERBERATED	PRODIGIOUSLY
BEAMS	DEMURENESS	SINUOUSLY	TRANSITORY	TEMPERAMENTAL

A Streetcar Named Desire Vocab

DESTITUTE	INDOLENT	REPROACH	MALARKEY	VOLUPTUOUSLY
IMMEASURABLY	UNCOUTH	INDECENT	INSUFFERABLY	LURID
PINION	CLEFT	FREE SPACE	RECKON	SUFFICIENT
SPECTRAL	BASHFUL	PERPETRATED	VIVID	PERPLEXITY
DIVESTED	COSMOPOLITAN	REFLECTIVELY	DOPE	EFFEMINATE

A Streetcar Named Desire Vocab

UNCOUTH	HUNCHED	PRIM	SWINDLE	TRANSITORY
MALARKEY	MENACING	PERPETRATED	REPERTOIRE	BESTIAL
HOARSELY	INCONGRUOUS	FREE SPACE	RETREATING	GAUDY
BASHFUL	DOPE	COSMOPOLITAN	SACCHARINE	LURID
GRAVELY	EXTRACTION	ANTIQUITY	PRIMITIVE	DESTITUTE

A Streetcar Named Desire Vocab

INEFFECTUAL	GOSSAMER	COARSE	REFLECTIVELY	VIVACITY
EFFEMINATE	BELLOWING	PORTIERES	SENTIMENTAL	ELATED
DEPLETION	PINION	FREE SPACE	EXPRESSIONS	CLEFT
SOLEMN	PRODIGIOUSLY	DEED	DIFFIDENT	REDOLENCE
GROTESQUE	INERT	DEMURENESS	TRANQUILITY	PERPLEXITY

A Streetcar Named Desire Vocab

INSUFFERABLY	VALISE	DIFFIDENT	EXTRACTION	INDECENT
PORTIERES	UNCAVALIER	GAUDY	INEFFECTUAL	DIVESTED
PRIMITIVE	SENTIMENTAL	FREE SPACE	TEMPERAMENTAL	MENACING
FEIGNED	UNCOUTH	VIVID	YEARNINGLY	REPERTOIRE
IMPROVIDENT	DEMURENESS	PRODIGIOUSLY	PRIM	BESTIAL

A Streetcar Named Desire Vocab

ANTIQUITY	SACCHARINE	REFLECTIVELY	VOLUPTUOUSLY	IMMEASURABLY
RAFFISH	PERPLEXITY	INDISTINGUISHABLE	SWINDLE	REVERBERATED
EFFEMINATE	CULTIVATED	FREE SPACE	GANDER	RETREATING
VIVACITY	COSMOPOLITAN	INCONGRUOUS	REDOLENCE	OMINOUSLY
SUFFICIENT	LAPPING	NOCTURNAL	BASHFUL	PITCH

A Streetcar Named Desire Vocab

DIVESTED	TRANQUILITY	NOTION	DEED	LAPPING
HETEROGENEOUS	IMMEASURABLY	GROTESQUE	UNCOUTH	INDECENT
PORTIERES	EFFEMINATE	FREE SPACE	REVERBERATED	COSMOPOLITAN
RECKON	CULTIVATED	IMPROVIDENT	SPECTRAL	BELLOWING
DEPLETION	VIVID	CALLOUS	GAUDY	SOLEMN

A Streetcar Named Desire Vocab

SINUOUSLY	MALARKEY	PITCH	CLEFT	ANTIQUITY
OMINOUSLY	SINISTER	GOSSAMER	DIFFIDENT	INCONGRUOUS
PERPETUAL	ELATED	FREE SPACE	REDOLENCE	INDIFFERENCE
TRANSITORY	INSUFFERABLY	PRIM	HECTIC	UNCAVALIER
YEARNINGLY	DOPE	PERPLEXITY	AMIABILITY	RETREATING

A Streetcar Named Desire Vocab

YEARNINGLY	BEAMS	INEFFECTUAL	SENTIMENTAL	CALLOUS
BASHFUL	TEMPERAMENTAL	ROW	CLEFT	PRIMITIVE
GRAVELY	RAFFISH	FREE SPACE	VIVID	GAUDY
MALARKEY	EXTRACTION	COARSE	REPROACH	TRANQUILITY
VALISE	EFFEMINATE	INDIFFERENCE	PRODIGIOUSLY	OMINOUSLY

A Streetcar Named Desire Vocab

REDOLENCE	SWINDLE	GANDER	UNCOUTH	HUNCHED
PORTIERES	HOARSELY	IMPROVIDENT	DESTITUTE	LAPPING
PITCH	LURID	FREE SPACE	VIVACITY	COMMON
REPERTOIRE	SOLEMN	SINUOUSLY	DIVESTED	SUFFICIENT
REVERBERATED	GROTESQUE	RHUMBA	PERPETRATED	MENACING

A Streetcar Named Desire Vocab

ROW	RHUMBA	BASHFUL	INCONGRUOUS	MENACING
REDOLENCE	COARSE	DESTITUTE	INSUFFERABLY	DOPE
PINION	REFLECTIVELY	FREE SPACE	UNCOUTH	FEIGNED
SPECTRAL	RECKON	RAFFISH	DIFFIDENT	GANDER
BEAMS	LAPPING	HOARSELY	BESTIAL	PRIM

A Streetcar Named Desire Vocab

GOSSAMER	SERENELY	INEFFECTUAL	SOLEMN	NOTION
NOCTURNAL	SWINDLE	EFFEMINATE	ELATED	INDECENT
PORTIERES	SUFFICIENT	FREE SPACE	SINUOUSLY	PERPETUAL
VIVACITY	UNCAVALIER	SENTIMENTAL	DIVESTED	RETREATING
DEED	HECTIC	IMPROVIDENT	IMMEASURABLY	MALARKEY

A Streetcar Named Desire Vocab

EXTRACTION	ANTIQUITY	SOLEMN	BASHFUL	FEIGNED
INDISTINGUISHABLE	NOCTURNAL	PERPETUAL	SERENELY	DEMURENESS
PORTIERES	PRIMITIVE	FREE SPACE	IMMEASURABLY	INDOLENT
TRANSITORY	BEAMS	REDOLENCE	SINUOUSLY	CULTIVATED
GOSSAMER	EXPRESSIONS	PERPLEXITY	TEMPERAMENTAL	RHUMBA

A Streetcar Named Desire Vocab

TRANQUILITY	VIVID	VALISE	COSMOPOLITAN	DEPLETION
IMPROVIDENT	DOPE	YEARNINGLY	ELATED	DESTITUTE
INERT	MALARKEY	FREE SPACE	INDIFFERENCE	PRODIGIOUSLY
INCONGRUOUS	SENTIMENTAL	UNCOUTH	VOLUPTUOUSLY	REFLECTIVELY
DIVESTED	BELLOWING	VIVACITY	HOARSELY	SINISTER

A Streetcar Named Desire Vocab

YEARNINGLY	PRIM	RETREATING	REPERTOIRE	BEAMS
GOSSAMER	UNCOUTH	SPECTRAL	INDISTINGUISHABLE	TEMPERAMENTAL
GROTESQUE	EXPRESSIONS	FREE SPACE	HUNCHED	COMMON
RAFFISH	COARSE	NOTION	REPROACH	DOPE
RHUMBA	VIVID	PERPETUAL	MENACING	EXHILARATION

A Streetcar Named Desire Vocab

REVERBERATED	IMMEASURABLY	LURID	DEMURENESS	SOLEMN
DEPLETION	INEFFECTUAL	VALISE	INERT	EXTRACTION
SINISTER	VIVACITY	FREE SPACE	SENTIMENTAL	INSUFFERABLY
HETEROGENEOUS	GRAVELY	INCONGRUOUS	NOCTURNAL	OMINOUSLY
DESTITUTE	TRANQUILITY	IMPROVIDENT	TRANSITORY	ELATED

A Streetcar Named Desire Vocab

BEAMS	INDOLENT	INSUFFERABLY	PRIM	PRIMITIVE
VIVACITY	YEARNINGLY	DOPE	DIFFIDENT	SINISTER
INDISTINGUISHABLE	OMINOUSLY	FREE SPACE	BASHFUL	HECTIC
EXTRACTION	RAFFISH	INEFFECTUAL	TRANSITORY	EFFEMINATE
INDIFFERENCE	HUNCHED	REFLECTIVELY	VIVID	INDECENT

A Streetcar Named Desire Vocab

INCONGRUOUS	EXPRESSIONS	PRODIGIOUSLY	DEPLETION	DEED
RECKON	NOTION	IMMEASURABLY	LURID	COARSE
SOLEMN	RETREATING	FREE SPACE	INERT	EXHILARATION
HOARSELY	REPERTOIRE	SINUOUSLY	NOCTURNAL	MALARKEY
IMPROVIDENT	MENACING	CLEFT	GOSSAMER	REDOLENCE

A Streetcar Named Desire Vocab

GANDER	MENACING	GAUDY	DEPLETION	PITCH
UNCAVALIER	INDOLENT	GROTESQUE	VOLUPTUOUSLY	VIVACITY
PERPLEXITY	REPERTOIRE	FREE SPACE	HUNCHED	CALLOUS
COSMOPOLITAN	SPECTRAL	RHUMBA	YEARNINGLY	SUFFICIENT
INDISTINGUISHABLE	PRIM	REDOLENCE	EXHILARATION	DEMURENESS

A Streetcar Named Desire Vocab

EFFEMINATE	REPROACH	FEIGNED	SINUOUSLY	PERPETUAL
DESTITUTE	HETEROGENEOUS	PRIMITIVE	TRANQUILITY	DIFFIDENT
PRODIGIOUSLY	RAFFISH	FREE SPACE	MALARKEY	BELLOWING
DEED	DOPE	CLEFT	ANTIQUITY	HECTIC
RETREATING	TRANSITORY	REVERBERATED	PINION	DIVESTED

A Streetcar Named Desire Vocab

REFLECTIVELY	NOCTURNAL	IMPROVIDENT	ANTIQUITY	RHUMBA
GANDER	DESTITUTE	EFFEMINATE	BEAMS	REPROACH
UNCOUTH	PERPETUAL	FREE SPACE	DEMURENESS	AMIABILITY
PRIM	BESTIAL	SWINDLE	LAPPING	TRANQUILITY
DEED	SOLEMN	BASHFUL	UNCAVALIER	RETREATING

A Streetcar Named Desire Vocab

REVERBERATED	COARSE	TRANSITORY	VIVACITY	INERT
CLEFT	DOPE	HUNCHED	INDOLENT	NOTION
PINION	EXHILARATION	FREE SPACE	SENTIMENTAL	REPERTOIRE
INSUFFERABLY	MENACING	LURID	GOSSAMER	MALARKEY
SINUOUSLY	HETEROGENEOUS	REDOLENCE	YEARNINGLY	CALLOUS

A Streetcar Named Desire Vocab

INERT	VIVACITY	REDOLENCE	TRANSITORY	IMPROVIDENT
SUFFICIENT	INDOLENT	COMMON	EXPRESSIONS	DIFFIDENT
SWINDLE	RAFFISH	FREE SPACE	EXTRACTION	AMIABILITY
INEFFECTUAL	UNCAVALIER	OMINOUSLY	GAUDY	YEARNINGLY
PRODIGIOUSLY	BASHFUL	SINUOUSLY	PERPETRATED	CULTIVATED

A Streetcar Named Desire Vocab

MALARKEY	EXHILARATION	NOCTURNAL	INDIFFERENCE	SOLEMN
HECTIC	RECKON	REVERBERATED	CALLOUS	GRAVELY
TEMPERAMENTAL	TRANQUILITY	FREE SPACE	NOTION	INDISTINGUISHABLE
INSUFFERABLY	LURID	PERPLEXITY	MENACING	VALISE
GANDER	HUNCHED	DOPE	BESTIAL	PITCH

A Streetcar Named Desire Vocab

INDOLENT	BELLOWING	INERT	DESTITUTE	LAPPING
UNCOUTH	ELATED	FEIGNED	TRANSITORY	DEPLETION
SINISTER	DIFFIDENT	FREE SPACE	CALLOUS	PORTIERES
PITCH	IMMEASURABLY	GROTESQUE	ANTIQUITY	RETREATING
GRAVELY	SACCHARINE	EXPRESSIONS	RHUMBA	HECTIC

A Streetcar Named Desire Vocab

MENACING	SPECTRAL	SERENELY	NOCTURNAL	COSMOPOLITAN
HOARSELY	GAUDY	REDOLENCE	PINION	TEMPERAMENTAL
DEMURENESS	ROW	FREE SPACE	BESTIAL	INDIFFERENCE
PRIM	REPROACH	AMIABILITY	PRODIGIOUSLY	CULTIVATED
DOPE	INEFFECTUAL	PRIMITIVE	EXTRACTION	INSUFFERABLY

www.ingramcontent.com/pod-product-compliance
Lightning Source LLC
Chambersburg PA
CBHW081450070526
44586CB00019B/2289